INDIFFERENT BOUNDARIES

MAPPINGS: Society/Theory/Space
A Guilford Series

Editors

Michael Dear
University of
Southern California

Derek Gregory
University of
British Columbia

Nigel Thrift
University of
Bristol

Indifferent Boundaries

SPATIAL CONCEPTS
OF HUMAN SUBJECTIVITY

Kathleen M. Kirby

THE GUILFORD PRESS
New York London

© 1996 The Guilford Press
A Division of Guilford Publications, Inc.
72 Spring Street, New York, NY 10012

Marketed and distributed outside North America by Longman Group
Limited

Printed in the United States of America

This book is printed on acid-free paper.

Last digit is print number: 9   7   6   5   4   3   2   1

Library of Congress Cataloging-in-Publication Data

Kirby, Kathleen M.
    Indifferent boundaries : spatial concepts of human subjectivity /
Kathleen M. Kirby.
        p.   cm.—(Mappings)
    Includes bibliographical references and index.
    ISBN 0-89862-903-9 (hardcover).—ISBN 0-89862-572-6 (pbk.)
    1. Subjectivity.   2. Space and time.   3. Feminist theory.
4. Psychoanalysis and philosophy.   5. Political science—Philosophy.
I. Title.   II. Series.
BD222.K57   1996
126—dc20   95-40223
                                                                   CIP

A much abbreviated version of Chapter One appeared as an essay entitled
"Thinking through the Boundary: The Politics of Location, Subjects, and
Space," in boundary 2, vol. 20, no. 2.

for my mother,
who always believed

Preface

"Space," an acquaintance might ask me when I mentioned the subject matter of my project. "You mean, like, outer space? 'The final frontier'?"

"No," I would explain, "like metaphors of space. Figures of space. And the role they play in discussions of subjectivity, of identity. Philosophers use the language of space all the time in their depictions of human nature. But nobody seems to be aware of their reliance on spatial language, and nobody looks into how that language structures their discussions."

"Oh," the interlocutor would reply. (I had lost him right around the time I used the word "subjectivity.") "I really love 'Star Trek.' Have you seen the episode about the Tribbles?"

The academic variation of this scene would differ only a little. "Space—you mean like nature writing? Pioneer narratives? Have you read Frederick Jackson Turner's *The Frontier in American History?* Now that I think about it, there *are* a lot of interesting spatial metaphors in American literature."

Well, yes, metaphors, but also—the real thing.

This project did begin with my studies in various Departments of English—my own academic "home" or point of origin—and it could be categorized as a work of literary theory. But it tends to maintain this testy grasp on, concern with, reality, and the actual movement of bodies and psyches through the physical structures in it. As the work reaches its destination, it appears to fit more comfortably into the category of "geography." This should probably be no great surprise, since geography is the field one might look to first to learn something about "space." I would guess, however, that to classical geographers, this study's fascination with representation, politics, and the psyche might appear a little out of bounds.

Indifferent Boundaries remains difficult to pin down, to locate. Part literary criticism and part geography, not quite history but not quite manifesto, definitely feminist and psychoanalytic but equally materialist and historical, never totally objective but only rarely autobiographical—the work exhibits, finally, the same obdurate elusiveness I attribute to space itself. *Space* is a slippery entity that filters through the screens between such categories as the psychic, the social, and the physical. It is an objective material and a site for inserting the subjective. It flows across the walls between the domain supposedly "inside" language and the world we imagine to be "outside" language. While I have not always been satisfied with this study's abilities to come to conclusions or to institute breaks between its topics, it mimics space in its scope, its versatility, and its range, and I suppose that is an acceptable mimicry.

Indifferent Boundaries is a work of fluidity and collision, aggregation and synthesis—an interdisciplinary work, a sample of cultural studies. A work of reconciliation (and only people who have known firsthand the disparities that exist in the field of cultural studies today—and between some of the thinkers I've studied—will catch the full weight of that term). When I first came to study the subject 5 or 10 years ago, I was, as one colleague has generously phrased it, "heavily under the sway of Althusserian Marxism." I was, at that time, committed to the idea prevalent in post-Althusserian and post-Foucauldian discourse that "subjects" could not be presumed to preexist any given interpellation, that is, any particular form that discourse or ideology might attempt to make them assume; they were totally and utterly the product of a given *énoncé,* of speech or technology. In the intervening years, I have studied a considerable amount of psychoanalytic theory and suffered some devastating personal losses. Together the two have convinced me that a more subtle and supple articulation of the subject is necessary.

I remain only tentatively convinced of the depiction of the unconscious, and opposed to the theory of engenderment, advanced by

Freud, Lacan, and their adherents, but I have found much of value in feminist reinterpretations of psychoanalytic doctrines and in object relations theory. Both struggle, it seems to me, with the difference between "inside" and "outside," selfhood and culture. My dissatisfaction with post-Althusserian notions of the subject comes from the fact that they seem to take up a wholly external position on the subject, giving the subject no depth, no internal grounding from which to react to culture's attempts to shape or form it.

My doubts were reinforced as I read Judith Butler's influential *Gender Trouble.* As ambitious and rigorous an argument as hers is—and as necessary as it may seem to a radical political theory—I am not certain we can do away altogether with the idea of the *persistence* of the subject, of a personal history, that lies beneath and sometimes subverts the discursive overtures directed toward any one material person. Paul Smith argues this point thoroughly in *Discerning the Subject,* where he calls for a more rounded, substantial conception of the subject. I will not repeat his argument here.

What I hope to contribute that is new is a capacity—albeit one that is self-conscious and critical—to view the subject through the lens of space, or to see how this focus is already operative. Space can be a site to bring together and understand the connections between the psychic and the social, the personal and the political.

I do not recommend that these categories be collapsed in a return to the philosophy of the individual and a liberal humanist political stance. I do see space, however, as a bridge between psychoanalysis and political theory, a means for mutual communication and complication that will keep either from becoming one-dimensional.

Acknowledgments

I am grateful to the Center for Twentieth Century Studies, the Department of English and Comparative Literature, and the Graduate School at the University of Wisconsin at Milwaukee; to Syracuse University; and to the University of New Hampshire. All these institutions provided financial support that made the completion of this project possible.

I owe personal thanks to Herbert Blau, Gregory Jay, and Kathleen Woodward, who helped to direct my exploration, often pushing me into areas where I might not otherwise have ventured; to Jane Gallop and Pani Norindr, who took the time to study what I found there; and to Felicity Nussbaum, Donald Morton, and Mas'ud Zavarzadeh, who provided the intellectual base that enabled my journey.

I also want to thank the fellow travelers who made the often difficult adventure more enjoyable: Karen Carr and Russell Potter, Julie and Robert Brown, Sandy Tweedie, Tracie Nadeau, Cynthia Wong, Cal Thomas, Christine Turczyn, Joy Rouse, and Roxann Wheeler. But my deepest gratitude is reserved for Michael James Collins, whose generous patience gave this journey meaning and whose love gives me a place to come home to.

Contents

Subjects in Space

VARIATIONS ON A THEME

The language of space is everywhere in theory today.[1] It "underwrites" current critical discussions: ideas about space form a kind of philosophical palimpsest for descriptions of politics, epistemology, and subjectivity; they are theory's substrate or foundation, upon which the whole critical edifice stands; but they also provide a kind of "guarantee," a solid referent outside language to which the intended line of argument can refer for stability, credibility, substantiality. At the same time, the language of space "overwrites" critical arguments, appearing as mere ornamentation or as dispensable rhetorical device. But even in such "supplemental" uses of spatial language, the idea of space to a degree "overdetermines."

Readers familiar with theory might immediately recognize the link with space in such critical phrases as "subject positioning" or "historical location," or in the proliferating projects planned to "map out" the cultural "terrain" or the political "field." One thinks immediately of the pioneering and influential work of Foucault, which so liberally borrows from the lexicon of space to posit a correlation between the forms of subjectivity, the mobile field of discourse, and the material

---

[1]Compare to the concluding sentence of Neil Smith and Cindi Katz's introductory paragraph in "Grounding Metaphor: Towards a Spatialized Politics": "The language of social and cultural investigation is increasingly suffused with spatial concepts in a way that would have been unimaginable two decades ago" (67). The authors go on to urge "enquiry concerning the implications of spatial metaphors" in order to advance a spatial politics (68). They also point out how the spatialization of theory—while seemingly helping to stabilize theoretical concepts—conversely also works to destabilize concepts of space (see Chapter One of this book).

effects of three-dimensional institutional spaces.[2] One might recall
from there the emphasis on "borderlands" or the arresting flexibility
of "center" and "margin" in critical texts concerned with issues of
national, racial, and cultural difference.[3] And, if one is familiar with
recent texts in cultural criticism, one might recognize the proliferation
of works that literally take space as their subject, for example, Edward
Soja's *Postmodern Geographies,* or the collection *Sexuality and Space,*
edited by Beatriz Colomina and published in the Princeton Papers
on Architecture series, or, to come even closer to the present, Derek
Gregory's inclusive study *Geographical Imaginations.*

Yet what might seem a "newfound" reliance on or attraction to
space—which could be dismissed as the result of trendiness—might
be instead a coming to the surface of, or a conscious and conscientious
exploration of, a theme that has been of vital significance to theory
for some time. Even when the importance of spatial concepts is not
made apparent by theory's specific use of words with spatial resonance,
theory, from Hegel and Saussure on up to Kristeva and Jameson, gains
much of its substance from concepts and metaphors that live in the
dimension of space. Both Hegel's master–slave dialectic and Saussure's
revision of linguistics depend upon the idea of division, the delineation
of two separate territories that persist in uneasy relation. Saussure's
linguistic theory argues that language functions by establishing a binary
difference within the massive, undefined, unorganized province of
language. Speech causes an opposition between binary terms to ma-
terialize and places them opposed across the abstract plane of language;
this distance precipitates meaning. Even theories that conceive of
language in terms of "reference" carry an embedded spatial foundation. "Reference" seems to imply that reality and language come in
two layers, or exist as two territories, with some magical interface
between them. The "word" and the "thing" occupy two bubbles, one
containing, for example, the word "tree" and the other a picture (or
idea, or real example) of the tree; an arrow leads from the first to
reassuringly designate the second.

---

[2]The signal Foucault texts on this topic would be *The Archaeology of Knowledge,
Discipline and Punish,* and *The History of Sexuality,* though themes of space, subject,
and discourse appear throughout his writing.

[3]Gloria Anzaldúa, in *Borderlands/La Frontera,* and bell hooks, in *Feminist Theory: From
Margin to Center,* made these terms part of the critical lexicon.

The idea of "difference" as opposed to "reference" put forth by Saussure provides the very basis of the current analytical enterprise. Contemporary political thought is much concerned with "difference," with *refiguring* difference, with *transfiguring* difference. To do so it often goes through space. How could it do otherwise? Difference itself seems a spatial concept, unimaginable or just barely imaginable outside the register of space. I do not know whether any other conceptualization of language, that is, one without the spatial overtones, is possible—particularly since, in writing, when language appears graphically in words, it does so on a plane or a medium constituted by space (as any example, from Lacan's gendered restrooms[4] to Cixous's provinces of masculine and feminine qualities, in the opening of "Sorties," will show). "Man" and "woman," "African" and "American," "mean" different things because they are in different places, separated on a page or a blackboard.

We could, to Derrida's discomfiture, turn away from space by turning from writing to speech. Speech too functions by difference, though its medium is temporal. Derrida's idea of *différance,* his emphasis on temporality, flux, and inconclusiveness, actually seems more pertinent to speech, though he frames it in the never-ending dialogue of writing. Even speech, however, seems to operate by the sequential activation of the spatial distances already present in the body of language. Lacan's theories of the subject likewise concern the de-formative effects of speech for the subject-coming-into-being—putting an emphasis on time, rather than space proper. His hypotheses on the subject resist being corralled within the stabilizing boundaries of space—as his disfiguring manipulations of graphemes and schemas demonstrates. These two thinkers unsettle the solidities of discourse and the subject by releasing them into the flux of time. This could, therefore, provide an especially rich and promising basis for reformulating political approaches. However, my subject here is space, and Lacan's and Derrida's permutations of space and time, while fascinating, provide a field far too complex to be encompassed in this short study.

Contemporary political writers have seen that the oppressive effects of "difference" result from its being configured as the rigid, exhaustive

---

[4]In Lacan, "The Agency of the Letter in the Unconscious or Reason since Freud."

division of a conceptual space that claims to represent natural divisions and eventually comes to construct material divisions (think of apartheid). In the older hierarchical model, difference is represented in the figure–ground relationship between a closed circle and an external unbounded plane. The full contents of the circle form an "inside," opposed to the "outside," which, being unarticulated and empty, conveniently figures as the site for receiving all of the rejects, the antitheses, of the interior (Freud's theory of the differentiation of the self conveniently represents and problematically reproduces this schema). The first move of political thought was to break this circle, equalizing the ontological and qualitative priorities of the two areas by making them adjacent but sundered territories. A more contemporary, but still problematic, definition of "difference" redefines it as the relation between two areas that are in-different, except for the fine line between them. Critics continue attempting to displace the oppressive effects of this spatial configuration, tinkering with the mechanics of "difference" in language that is more or less comparable to space. They reverse the hierarchy of terms, shifting the figure–ground relation of "center" and "margin"; they multiply boundaries, and thereby territories, fragmenting the unity of either area into many discrete bounded entities; they blur the boundary, or complicate it by transporting parcels of one area into the territory of the other. In relation to gender, the first move, to equalize territories, is apparent in liberal humanist and feminist attempts to achieve the simple equation of women and men. Alternately, cultural feminists strive to overturn the gender hierarchy and to reclaim "feminine" traits—thereby demonstrating a desire to reverse the figure–ground relationship. The popular women's movement points out the sociological dispersion of traits labeled "masculine" and "feminine" across populations "male" and "female"—thus relying on the "osmotic" mode. Feminists interested in national, cultural, and racial difference, using the multiplicatory approach, fragment the unity of the pristine categories of "man" and "woman." Feminists using ideology critique start with the assumption that all gender differentiations are culturally effected; hence they radically desubstantialize and temporize the gender boundary, negating its "natural" authority and erasing its metaphysical priority. I have chosen texts that work through these possibilities in directly spatial language. Many others do not, but I would claim that even in texts without immediate spatial connotations, a deployment of or an underlying dependence on a spatial schematic is evident. As I suggested above, it is not clear that the spatialization of "difference" is not itself the problem (space implying endurance), but the persistence of this theme, the reason for the critical recourse to it, has yet to be explored. Clearly it offers *something*: the issue would be to separate out its beneficial uses from its deleterious ones.

The reliance on space comes, in part, from the relative paucity of language. Though post-Saussurian theorists have worked to loosen the link between "language" and "the real" (or at least to reverse it), our language is nonetheless predicated on, and enabled by, an idea of correspondence of words to "things"—to objects, which are necessarily dimensional and necessarily exist in space, even when this substantiality appears only in the dimensionality of signifieds. Words take shape. Theory, in overburdening language or squeezing it for its fullest signifying capacities, makes the materiality of the signified more prominent. The affection that so many critical discourses demonstrate toward the language of space also derives from its popularity in everyday speech, but there spatial metaphors rarely take on the same embodiment. We speak of our "political positions" and our "personal space," but our everyday use of spatial tropes seems less serious: we maintain a mental separation between the two worlds of expression and reality, allow words to dance over the surface of their unexplored implications, and are less likely to build them into significant dimension. In theory, it is a different story. Metaphors of space take on a sneaky kind of three-dimensionality and referentiality, whether unbidden or intended. Revealing the underlying fabric of spatiality in a work—even one that does not seem to refer to a realm immediately recognizable as "spatial"—can be a very effective method of revealing the underlying theoretical assumptions of its argument.[5]

At times, as I have mentioned, we do employ figures of space only ornamentally, or as rhetorical figures meant to illustrate an argument. I will be concerned throughout this work with separating tropes of space that function gratuitously from those that serve a more substan-

[5]For a similar consideration, see David Harvey, "From Space to Place and Back Again: Reflections on the Condition of Postmodernity": "The ambiguity and the multiple layers of meanings . . . suggests, perhaps, some underlying unity which, if we can approach it right, will reveal a great deal about social, political and spatial practices in interrelation with each other" (4).

tial, or substantiating, purpose. For the transaction with space is *not* one of mere—or simple—metaphor (I bow here to Derrida), one that theory could easily do without. Frequently, there is a shading off into indeterminacy between the spatial words that function decoratively and a more fundamental use of space. Theorists themselves often seem uncertain about whether they are speaking of *real space,* and practices taking place within it, or of a realm purely discursive—this may be the case with Fredric Jameson's work on mapping. And sometimes, as I will show with the work of Freud, a space that begins as a mere descriptive convenience may turn into a space with referential autonomy: in describing the space of the psyche, language gathers a material weight and body. It tends to become real—and may be the only reality we have.

⊶ ⊷

This book combines three distinct but interrelated projects: one interpretive, one historical, and one polemical. First, it seeks to analyze the language of space and the use that theorists of the subject, from Sigmund Freud to Fredric Jameson and Adrienne Rich, have made of it. Second, it describes changes that have taken place in space—both real and conceptual—from the Renaissance to the postmodern era. Third, the book follows its own inquiry into the "space of the subject," measuring the validity of spatial approaches to subjectivity and considering their political potential. It argues that the plasticity that has afflicted space since the modern period has brought about new possibilities for liberation for postmodern subjects, and indicates the ways in which contemporary critical/political writers have attempted to harness this new malleability in the "space of the subject." The three lines of argument develop concurrently in each chapter. The material is divided thematically, with each chapter taking up a particular problematic, and gathering sites and sources appropriate to resituating the issues.

Some of the questions it addresses include: When theorists use the language of space, what do they mean? In what ways are subjects the effects of spaces? In what meaningful sense can we speak of a "space of the subject"? Is subjectivity, literally, a spatial phenomenon? Has the consistency of space changed between the Enlightenment and the postmodern periods? Has subjectivity undergone collateral transformations? If, as many critics argue, the postmodern period is one characterized by spatial flux and uncertainty, can this plasticity provide radical possibilities for the reformation of political subjects? And what, if any, practical relation does this abstract theoretical discussion have to the real political relationships we contemporary subjects live on a daily basis?

Chapter One, "Defining the Space of the Subject: Investigating the Boundaries of Feminism," circulates around a discussion of "the politics of location" and the function of that term for two feminist critics, Adrienne Rich and Chandra Talpade Mohanty. This chapter lays some terminological groundwork, and interrogates the interrelation of numerous registers of space in the constitution of subjects: geopolitical, semiotic, somatic, and psychic. I note that the new emphasis on space might derive from the combination of politicized with poststructural theory; space helps us to recognize that "subjects" are determined by their anchoring within particular bodies or countries. At the same time, space in the abstract maintains a fluidity, a revisability, that appeals to the reformative impulses of today. Contemporary theory has landed on the *boundary* as the site for preserving while refiguring difference. The remaining chapters develop this theme, considering the history and the future of subjective confines.

Chapter Two, "Lost in Space: Establishing the Limits of Identity," delves immediately into the conflict between rigidity and fluidity in space by offering a comparative treatment of Renaissance and postmodern mapping. Its main theoretical point is that there is a definite relation between the kind of space occupied by the subject and the form the subject takes. The chapter compares the form of subjectivity evident in Enlightenment individualism to that of the postmodern *sujet en procès* (roughly, the subject "in process/on trial") by comparing the journals of two early American explorers, Cabeza de Vaca and Samuel Champlain, to the journal of a contemporary cultural pioneer, Fredric Jameson. Both rely on mapping: Jameson for progressive purposes, the explorers for colonial ends. But given that Jameson relies on the technology of mapping, his praxis maintains the rigid, uncompromising outlines of the Enlightenment individual. Thus his project of "cognitive mapping" remains an exclusionary practice. The chapter demonstrates that political practices are allied with spatial matrices and the differing kinds of subjectivities they might generate.

Where Chapter Two skips from the Renaissance to the postmodern worlds, Chapter Three lingers in the modern period to uncover the roots of the supposedly *post*modern fluidity of space. "Freudian Fabrications: De-forming Modern Spaces" once again draws parallels between real and theoretical configurations of space, reading in Freud's descriptions of the subject the symptoms of the modern deterioration of space. The source of the modern subject's anxiously permeable nature are found in transformations in real space wrought by technology, urbanization, and the collapse of colonialism. Around the turn of the century, "everything solid melt[ed] into air," as Marx observed—including space, including subjectivity. The "waning" of the material, as one might call it, left room for language to be perceived as a much more palpable, productive force on the social scene. Is the subject really a space? The language used to describe it makes it be lived as such, giving it the force of the real. Hence Freud's semiosis enabled, and continues to enable, new mutations in subjectivity.

Chapter Four, "Vertigo: Postmodern Spaces and the Politics of the Subject," undertakes an intensive engagement with poststructural philosophy from figures such as Michel de Certeau, Gilles Deleuze, Michel Foucault, and Jane Gallop, focusing, once again, on their engagements with space. The chapter analyzes why the figuration and refiguration of space might have become such an important element of these writers' projects. Working from the Freudian analytic framework established in the previous chapter, I argue that these theorists view the real—that is, external space—as a precipitate of the division between the inside and the outside of the subject. Deforming inner and outer space and the relation between them allows these critics to imagine ways in which individual subjects might take a larger hand in the formation of this external reality. The impetus for refiguring space in this body of writing might come, in fact, from a sense on the part of these historical subjects of a mismatch between inside and outside, desire and reality. However, I challenge their frequent conclusion that an individual reconfiguration of space might be adequate to transforming the social landscape, proposing instead that such a transformation can only come from a broader metamorphosis of the shared, extrapersonal realm.

Taking seriously, however, the poststructural contention that language is a filter that forms the reality that passes through it, I conclude by examining one example of representation, and how changes in it have quite literally changed the "space of the subject." In Chapter

Five, "Indecent Exposure: Redefining the Spaces of Gender," I look at the legal and popular discourses surrounding the act of indecent exposure and how they both reflect and inflect the forms of gendered subjectivity. This chapter builds on the theory of "the gaze" developed by feminist film critics, object relations psychoanalysts, and feminist psychoanalytic critics. In the constitution of gendered subjectivity, physical and psychic contours overlap. "Masculine" and "feminine" identities, I suggest, are the effects of qualitatively different forms of space, with the masculine occupying a securely bounded and expansive space, and the feminine taking a porous, flexible form. It is in the juxtaposition of these complementary but contrasting spaces that female violation occurs. But the forms that subjectivities take are, poststructural thought indicates, malleable—subject to the reformative powers of representation. I conclude that the shapes gendered subjects take must be reformed if we are to achieve an equitable social environment. The book attempts to integrate theoretical and practical (political) concerns, with Chapter Five providing one representative case study.

⊷─⊠✦⊠─⊶

What business do we, who work with language, have in discussing space and spatial practices? What function does such a tropology play for us? What does it offer us? How is it limiting?

This study aims to address the difficult questions that lie at the heart of the critical investment in space. It is a work of literary theory, and therefore has as its first concern the analysis of language. However, a large part of my argument is that the theoretical turn to space stems from the delicate reference that category promises with concrete reality. Each chapter attempts to hold onto real space, not evacuating the material referent in order to indulge in joyful play with the metaphor. Throughout I maintain external, three-dimensional space, and the actions taking place within it, as a touchstone, measuring the validity of theoretical assertions in relation to the experiences of real subjects in space, especially my own. It may turn out that "experience" itself cannot be separated from precise places and spaces. While that quality has been one reason theorists in the antiphenomenological vein have turned against it, I see the materiality of experience as precisely the quality that makes us unable to do without it, for theoretical purposes. It is what remains to remind us that our theories *do make* a difference; that we are talking about real people, in a real world, and trying to change it. The *language* of space, because of its apparently material reference, seems to close the gap between these two worlds, giving contemporary theory an avenue for (imagining) affecting the real.

CHAPTER ONE

Defining the Space of the Subject

INVESTIGATING THE BOUNDARIES OF FEMINISM

"The space of the subject": what could the phrase mean, or be made to mean?

The first category of space that might spring to mind is physical space, space as we usually think of it, the three-dimensional space that people occupy. The largest and, at least at first glance, most easily quantifiable aspect of physical space is geography, the expanse of the material world and its features.

The space of nation has become, in the last decade, a primary figure in debates about the politics of the subject. Subjects exist within particular places, with identifiable physical coordinates. Our place of birth does much to determine us as subjects, giving us a native tongue (or perhaps bilingualism), often a religious commitment, a race, and a particular structure of gender and race. National origins predetermine ideological formations; individual cultures, set apart by the bounds of continents and countries, rivers and mountains, form their realities in divergent ways. As subjects, we vary widely depending on the actual *place* we came from and the subsequent *places* we occupy.

Physical space also makes a difference on a smaller scale. There are the (psychologically, culturally, and physically) separate worlds of "country" and "city," with suburbia sometimes acting as a transition zone between the two or sometimes existing as a third separate world.

Cities and towns have "good" neighborhoods and "bad" ones, which have impact on us in different ways, and which we negotiate differently. Minnie Bruce Pratt has poetically and usefully considered the phenomenon of personal location in "Identity: Skin Blood Heart." Space and where we are in it, she points out, determines a large portion of our status as subjects, and obversely, the kinds of subjects we are largely dictates our degree of mobility and our possible future locations. As a middle-class and well-educated white person I usually live in the elite bohemian districts of cities, largely residential areas dotted with coffee shops and upscale book and gift stores. Because of my color, I tend to avoid predominately nonwhite areas, often more to avoid rejection than to avoid violence, but also to avoid (unthinkingly) carrying on the tradition of imperialism in pursuit of personal pleasures. And as a woman, I avoid going to a lot of places, especially when I am alone at night.

The space we occupy interacts with what could be considered another space, the space of the body. Between them our consciousness often mediates, making decisions about the kind of space it wants to enter and changing form to adapt to the situations in which it finds itself. We often think of our bodies as spaces composed of depth and surface, interior and exterior, with their contents properly contained within a skin, hermetically sealed and closed off from the environment.[1] "The term 'space' refers to very different concepts," writes Claudine Herrmann in a passage that has always intrigued me: "There is a physical and a mental space for everyone. These two categories have in common the capacity to be invaded: one by violence, the other by indiscretion" ("Women in Space and Time" 168). Perhaps in speaking of the space of the body, the female subject has more at stake than the male; our vaginas, our wombs, our menstruations, and our pregnancies make the interiority of our bodies seem much more present, obvious, conscious, critical. We all eat and shit, but are these functions peripheral? At the edges of the body and of consciousness?

---

[1] All of Kristeva's work, of course, has served to problematize this clean distinction by focusing on areas of passage—mouth, anus, urethra, vagina—that produce confusion and anxiety for the subject attempting to pretend its autonomy. See especially *Powers of Horror*. Luce Irigaray also problematizes this model of interiority and exteriority in "This Sex Which Is Not One," as does Jane Gallop in the introduction to *Reading Lacan*.

For me, these bodily functions are ephemeral processes; they might generate a dimensional body image, but one that is at best fragmented, one that barely penetrates the surface. My sexuality centers my bodily consciousness, making an open berth for me to occupy as a specifically female subject. (The legal apparatus likewise uses my sex to define my body as an open space, a potential container or vessel whose interiority, though central to me as a female subject, also links with the public domain. Hence while my sexuality *centers* my individual female consciousness, it also *fragments,* or tears apart, my subjectivity, to allow me to be woven into a larger ideological complex.) Though subjects of all races, classes, and ethnicities may live their bodies as volumes, for subjects from marginal groups the *margins* of the body may prove more palpable, central, defining, and affecting. If I live my body as volume, my "femininity," my gender, resides at its surface, on the level of the clothes I wear or the lipstick I (do or don't) apply. My race occurs likewise at the surface. The surfaces of our bodies interact with the divisions between groups drawn up by ideology, and as Herrmann indicates, it is precisely when the space of the body coincides with the space of ideology that violence can occur.

Speaking of the social effect of different kinds of bodies leads us to another "space" in which the subject could be located: the abstract but mappable space of discursive terrains. Words, which exist only as intangible, one-dimensional temporal strings, manage, in our culture, to divide up and constitute conceptual and social space. Binary pairs of words operate on a center–margin logic, setting up borders delimiting social groups. "White" becomes not a term but a community, evicting the "black" (and the "yellow," the "brown," and the "red").

Such patterns of belonging and excluding may function in the first instance only to divide conceptual space, but they finally operate materially, structuring physical spaces (think of the slave's quarters and the master's house, or of who usually lives in the pricey townhouses and who in the ghetto), and discursively, defining politically operative laws to material effect (think of the laws defining "race" in themselves). They give us individual and social form. As Teresa de Lauretis puts it so eloquently in *Technologies of Gender,* the term "woman" clings to us "like a wet silk dress" (12). Words such as "black" and "white," "rich" and "poor," "man" and "woman," "straight" and "queer," clothe us, define us, determine what we can and can't do, where we can and can't go. They are constraining enclosures we seek to vault as well as, often, a ground for identity that we take up purposely, for personal and political reasons.

Words may give us social form; they also offer an at-least-partial-container for identity. Before, below, or beside this semiotic shape of identity, reinforcing or resisting our cultural placement, is another space of the subject, the space of subjectivity. We have a long tradition (reinforced by psychoanalysis) of speaking of the psyche itself as a space. Freud designed numerous topographies for the id, the ego, and the superego, and for the unconscious, the preconscious, the conscious, and the repressed, but his schemata sometimes did and sometimes did not correspond to a space of which he thought the psyche a manifestation. Lacan considers the ego a phantasmic space, a strictly fictional projection of unconscious processes that are "structured like a language,"[2] which is to say, not structured in space at all. Freud gives more credit, on some occasions, to the idea of the spatial psyche. The ego, like a container, incorporates the sense of the body's surface, taking on dimensional form.

But at other times, it is not for Freud just the function "ego" but the whole subject that exhibits a spatial framework. (I will be investigating this paradigm in a reading of *Beyond the Pleasure Principle* and *Civilization and Its Discontents* in Chapter Three.) Lacan, though he subjects the space of the subject to a schismatic torsion, also—at least in his early work—deems space a central category in the formation of the subject. In the well-known essay "The Mirror Stage," "I" is the structure framed by the inverted gaze of the infant's "eye" apprehending its displaced image. Though it is effected by a convoluted space, one based not on centrality inside a boundary but on alienation across a break, the subject is nonetheless tenable only as a result of space.

But we do not need to review the psychoanalytic literature to posit a "psychic space." In everyday speech, space offers one of the most common tropes for psychic existence. We speak of feelings occurring "deep inside" and regularly distinguish between surface (how we appear) and depth (how we "really feel"). Lacan will lead us, however, to the final "space of the subject" I wish to explore. This is what

---

[2]This thesis summarizes Lacan's work, but I find it explicitly enunciated in only one place: "The Freudian Unconscious and Ours," *The Four Fundamental Concepts of Psycho-Analysis*, 20.

might be called "social" space, a kind of space conveniently bringing together the others I have adumbrated above, themselves interconnected. Kaja Silverman, in *The Acoustic Mirror,* points out that subjectivity, for Lacan, occurs not only when the subject incorporates its own displaced image, but also when it is incorporated as an image by another. The second moment is required for subjectification (in both senses—the subject comes into being at the same moment that it becomes subjected) to occur. Such instantiations of the subject take place in real space, in the network of paths and buildings and parks and sidewalks and hallways we traverse daily. Though other sensory dimensions also play a part in our organization of the subjective landscape (is it not *smell* as well as *sight* that elicits our physical positioning toward vagrants—or babies?), sight provides probably the most telling and sensitive mechanism for dividing up, and locating ourselves in, the social field.

We see, and this is one moment of consciousness; our psyches spread out indiscriminately, engulfing the whole object world. Our existence is unlimited, coterminous with (usually) our vision. It takes little more than a hoot, a whistle, a "Hey, you!" or the noticed gaze (hostile or admiring) of another to force us to contract into a much more limited space, one that correlates more or less with the body, that is marked by cultural divisions coinciding with those in discourses of race, class, gender, and nation. Althusser's parable of hailing, in "Ideology and Ideological State Apparatuses," provides a perfect allegory. A cop yells "Hey, you!" and though I may not be particularly guilty, I know when I am the one intended. I *take my place.* Interactions in social space bring into articulation psychic frontiers and bodily surfaces, social and discursive outlines, and the seams of the fabric of physical spaces.

Thus we could define a space of the subject on a number of different levels. In speaking of the subject we will want to take into account topological, geopolitical, corporeal, psychic, discursive, and social spaces. The preceding act of defining makes it clear that divisions between these registers of space often will not hold, yet neither can the "space of the subject" be marshalled into one decisive format. If the body takes form in that three-dimensional landscape of the object-world, geography tends to be understood in terms of a two-dimensional material surface, and language in the one-dimensional, temporal plane in which linguistic binaries are continually reconstituted. Each of these spaces shapes the subject's "substance" according

to different logics, and each space offers its own degree of freedom
and imposes its own kind of confinement. Space itself is rather shifty.[3]
Defining normally has to do with fixing a territory and demarcating
its edges, with orienting ourselves in a stabilized environment. Defining space for the purposes of discussing the subject might instead tend
to demonstrate just how flexible space can be.

To illustrate, let's look more closely at geography. Geography might
seem like one of the most apparent, even transparent, coordinates of
subjective location, but as the critics I focus on in this chapter will
demonstrate, it is far from being a secure marker. In previous centuries,
perhaps, geopolitical borders safely contained people, so that they
could identify themselves with the outlines of defined places. With
the explosive growth in transportation and communication technologies over the past century, however, the physics of identity have
become considerably more complex. Subjects, at least those of certain
classes, circulate flexibly across the territorial outlines of home countries, states, and cities.[4] One need not look to "America" to find an
"American"; one might instead look to China, or to Nepal.

Beginning to name countries makes it clear that the "dislocation"
we often associate with postmodernism has been developing for at
least three or four centuries (and has always been driven by economic

[3]Derek Gregory captures well the shifty reference of space in his discussion of "the
politics of location." This phrase, he writes, "is intended to have a much wider meaning
than the conventionally geographic, to be sure, but it is also more than a literary
trope." See his *Geographical Imaginations,* 126.

[4]Postmodernism is increasingly interpreted as a symptom in the West of a global
torsion of space caused by the transformation of first and third world economic
relations. Fredric Jameson links the two successfully in the interview with Anders
Stephanson in Andrew Ross, ed., *Universal Abandon?* Numerous other critics, among
them Laura Kipnis, in "Feminism: The Political Conscience of Postmodernism?" (also
in *Universal Abandon?*), Roger Rouse, in "Mexican Migration and the Social Space
of Postmodernism," and Jose David Saldivar, in "Chicano Studies on the Border"
have made the argument that late capitalism has splintered former geographic entities,
transgressing the pseudohermetic frontiers that might once have comfortably
contained national identities, ethnic categories, and the tripartite economic process
of need, production, consumption. As symbiotic relations break down the distinctions
between some territories of the world, on other fronts, former totalities splinter (back)
into jostling ethnic and political fragments, "the repressed returning in fervent or
savage forms" (Herbert Blau, personal communication). For now, the hierarchy
between first and third world remains, but it will be interesting to discover whether
even this situation will change, now that third world peoples and nations are beginning
to find a space for self-representation on the world scene.

repositioning). But what has (almost) always been an economic fact is now being felt intensely as well on an individual psychic scale and is being acknowledged (or symptomatized) in cultural productions worldwide. Fredric Jameson and others argue that Western subjectivity in the late capitalist world—no longer able to ignore its situation vis-à-vis global economic interdependency—must begin to grapple with its confusing interconnectedness.

When we speak of the space of the subject in terms of geography, it is clear that we are not strictly referring to transparent, identifiable, self-evident physical space. We are referring to cultural coordinates, national and regional commitments, which, though they may refer to a place, are not confined to it and can be (and often must be) preserved outside its bounds or shaped to fit different parameters. Geography as an index of subjects ceases to be the dependable anchor of certain subjective traits and becomes more like the medium for measuring difference and distance, proximity and similarity.

Finally, we come to ask whether "geography" itself is so stable: countries are defined in binary or multiplicity by borders that are more or less conventional, fragmentary, temporal, and subject to trans- formation on a diplomatic, military, and personal scale—just like the borders of subjects themselves. Transgressing or eliminating these bor- ders may be offered, in both personal and geopolitical schemas, as one of the primary and necessary steps in a journey to utopia, but just as often such breaches of the walls of "propriety" or ownership occasion dispute, disaster, or the annihilation of one of the "participating" parties. I hope it would not be vulgar to compare the dispersion of the Soviet empire and the phenomenon of date rape, two topics that achieved prominence in the American media at about the same time, to punctuate my point: the fragility of the borders constructing identity is as much their problem as their promise, and given the endurance of the desires, hatreds, or histories they contain, reforming them may not be the guaranteed path toward political paradise.

It's already clear, from this brief discussion of geography, that de- fining the subject in terms of space isn't going to *settle* anything, isn't going to make matters simpler or easier to resolve. Why, then, are so many critics wholeheartedly taking up the problematics of space? Precisely because of its complexity and inclusive capacity. Space can form a medium for reconnecting us with the material while preserving a fluidity to subjective boundaries. It brings together the quantifiable and the qualifiable, the material and the abstract, the body and the mind, the outside and the inside. We locate our perceptions outside in it, and inside ourselves. It is our environment, it links us to our environment, and it also seems to fortify a distinction between self and environment, girding (and guarding) an interiority. It is itself the medium of interconnection and difference, measurement, similarity, and distance, markers that become important in evaluating the possibilities of coalition, or the importance of separatism.

Perhaps the present-day efflorescence of spatial approaches to the subject has one main root: once we discard the Enlightenment notion of the individual as disembodied, evanescent, transcendent "mind," it is impossible to imagine the subject except in some yet-to-be-specified relation to real space. We can't overlook, non-Western and nonwhite critics attest, the difference that occupying different geographical or cultural spaces can forge in making what might have seemed like abstract, "objective," unlocated evaluations. Further, feminist critics have recognized how critical the daily interaction of subjects and their bodies in social spaces can be. The subject and its form, subjects and their natures, are tied into political commitments and ethical positions by virtue of being tied into particular material spaces, like bodies or countries, ghettos or suburbs, kitchens or boardrooms. Yet space maintains a certain fluidity, a mobility: if we are speaking of space in the abstract, it is susceptible to folding, division, reshaping. A space persists only as long as the boundary creating it is deliberately maintained, and the spaces these boundaries encircle are subject to continual remodeling. Hence the optimism and anxiety of space in relation to identity in the modern, or postmodern, world. Recent criticism has taken up space as a flexible medium for marking out the properties of subjects without getting mired in organic essentialisms or evaporating the concrete significance of political interests. Two essays from the last decade, Adrienne Rich's "Notes toward a Politics of Location" (1984) and Chandra Talpade Mohanty's "Feminist Encounters: Locating the Politics of Experience" (1987) can help us begin to evaluate the multiple forms the "space of the subject" might take. Rich's essay introduced the theme of the "politics of location" that now saturates feminist theory, especially postimperial feminism. While Mohanty relies on Rich as conceptual precursor, her work, particularly her more recent "Cartographies of Struggle" (1991), positions itself as a refinement of the theoretical capacities of spatial tropes.

Mohanty tends to view the space of the subject as objective and impersonal, while Rich seeks to occupy and personalize it. Mohanty foregrounds the importance of geography; Rich moves more fluidly through a number of registers of space. Throughout the following discussion I will be evaluating the differences in their spatial tropographies, yet from the outset I want to emphasize certain similarities. Both Rich and Mohanty are seeking a responsive and responsible[5] way for speaking about the subject, with each attempting to define the *points de capiton* (connecting points) between physical place and the more intangible parameters of being: subject positions in discourse and political and personal identity. Each attempts to mediate the difference between space and place. *Place* seems to assume set boundaries that one fills to achieve a solid identity. Place settles space into objects, working to inscribe the Cartesian monad and the autonomous ego. It perpetuates the fixed parameters of ontological categories, making them coherent containers of essences, in relation to which one must be "inside" or "outside," "native" or "foreign," in the same way that one can, in the Euclidean universe at least, be in only one place at one time. If place is organic and stable, space is malleable, a fabric of continually shifting sites and boundaries. The two authors try to negotiate the relations between space and place, maintaining place in order to foreground the materiality of subjectivity, but investing in space to demonstrate and promote the subject's mutability. They seek to grant a plasticity to the subject but avoid making it no more than the unfettered echo bouncing around in a textual chasm. To negotiate space and place, to arbitrate materiality and mutability, and, most importantly, to locate themselves personally in subjectivity, Rich and Mohanty migrate from space itself to its edges, landing on the boundary as the site for reform.

For Mohanty, the subject's space is flat and fleeting, momentary and abstract, temporary and empty. Subjects are relatively discontinuous from one moment to the next, and the different aspects of any given individual—in terms of race, class, or gender character—do not necessarily align.

Mohanty's use of spatial coordinates presents itself, at first glance, as nothing more than a figurative device; Mohanty makes spatial tropes

---

[5]I wish to thank Joy Rouse for sharing her thoughts on "responsibility" with me, and for her careful and considerate reading of this chapter.

a heavily marked vehicle for her rhetorical purposes. Yet they lead to an underlying spatial foundation for her concept of subjectivity that I find quite revealing about the politics she advocates. Discourse theory, rapidly developing on the heels of Foucault and Althusser, has insisted that the spaces laid out for us by culture can be farflung, leaving us dispersed positionalities that will not necessarily connect up with each other or with the body. Further, the movement to eradicate essentialism, particularly in feminist theory, has made it an error to align the edges of socially constructed subject positions with the margins of the body, that is, to assume that the positions mapped out by physical space coincide with those created within discursive systems.[6] Mohanty's work registers a preference for the atomized, sectored kind of space underlying both these approaches to the subject. Her "space of the subject" is a flat space that can be mapped on the terrain of discursive relations or a fleeting intersection of conflicting political initiatives. Her reliance on metaphors from cartography and geography indicates this underlying philosophical terrain, the idea that theory's point is to identify the location of the subject within systems that exceed the individual.

Mohanty is far from unaware of the implications of the tropology she advances; her space of the subject is part and parcel of the politics she advocates. Nonetheless, examining her uses of space more thoroughly will allow me to begin showing the interrelations of figurative spaces, concepts of subjectivity, and political perspectives; Mohanty's work provides an excellent grounding for examining and pressuring one perspective on the subject frequently traced out in theory today.

Mohanty resists the idea of an organic, rounded subject, and therefore rejects all of the interiority implied by vessels and containing structures. She praises Bernice Johnson Reagon's "Coalition Politics" because of Reagon's resistance to the "insider" status of home in advancing a coalition. For Reagon, as Mohanty reads her, coalition is "opposed, by definition, to home" ("Encounters" 39). Quite in con-

---

[6]Does this trend to evaporate the space of the subject indicate less a desire for descriptive precision than a wish by women to escape the position culture assigns us? "No, not me, I am not that, what you say I am. . . ." We seek to extricate our bodies from the uses to which culture tries to put them, and to extricate our *selves* from the inscriptions culture has tied to our bodies. I share in this wish, but wish too that this motive could be more manifestly acknowledged; that we could erase the masculinist patterns on the container rather than smash it altogether.

trast to Rich, Mohanty refuses organic and dimensional models of subjectivity. She brings in "home"—that walled site of belonging— only to negate it.[7] Mohanty commends Reagon likewise for her insistence on "*strategic* locations and positionings" ("Encounters" 39). One cannot be *inside* a coalition because coalition is not based on the assumption of interiority underlying organicist definitions of political interests. In "Cartographies of Struggle," Mohanty avoids positing "biological" or even "sociological" constituencies, preferring a solely "political" one (7). The things that link women together into a political movement are not the similarities of their existing internal qualities, but instead the external features of political activity. We are determined by the place we're in, and not vice versa. Subjectivity is framed in opposition to a political move on the part of the hegemonic system. For Mohanty, "subjectivity" is a collection of widely scattered points whose existence is guaranteed only in the momentary action of a discursive instance.

Mohanty does not see gender as inhering within the bounds of already constituted persons. In "Cartographies of Struggle," Mohanty avers that her own "locations" are "discontinuous" (3) not only because of the obvious contradiction in the fact that she is both "of" the third world and "of" the United States, but also because her status as, say, woman, does not pass intact across these cultural boundaries. In "Feminist Encounters," she notes that "gender is *produced* as well as uncovered in feminist discourse, and definitions of experience, with attendant notions of unity and difference, form the very basis of this production" (32). (Gender here is located in discourse, rather than in persons; I might counter by arguing that while gender positionalities are produced by discourse, gender itself is lived, both inside and outside the self.) She goes on to say that "the unity of women is best understood not as *given,* on the basis of a natural/psychological commonality; it is something that has to be worked for, struggled towards—*in history*" (38, italics in original). She is seeking to remove femininity from the solid ontological terrain and to activate it in the transitory, temporal process of language.

---

[7]Mohanty joins Biddy Martin in a more complex and satisfying rendering of "home" in "Feminist Politics: What's Home Got to Do with It?" an analysis of Minnie Bruce Pratt's "Identity: Skin Blood Heart."

The psychological, a space traditionally inseparable from ideas of dimensionality and persistence, falls outside the bounds of Mohanty's interests. Mohanty criticizes Robin Morgan's view of experience in "Planetary Feminism" as, on the one hand, entirely personal, or, on the other, as fundamentally general ("located in women as a pre-constituted collective"; "Encounters" 37). She seeks to disengage the psychological from the cultural—the "psychological" is conflated with the "essential," a category she repudiates. The interiority of the category "woman," and therefore the interiority of the subjects labeled "woman," cannot be assumed, but exists only in moments of social construction.

Mohanty sees the subject as a potential collection of noncorrelating positions. At the same time, she wishes to maintain before the Western (feminist) view the specificity of (women) subjects of other cultures. Geography plays a primary but contradictory role for her: it represents the empty markers of ethnic and gender positions in the global dialogue, but it also points out the real presence of "others" and their intransigent bodies. Geography indicates, incongruously, both the insubstantiality and the actuality of subjects.

Mohanty wishes to fortify the Western feminist recognition of the existence of non-Western women and to pinpoint the consequences of occupying particular locations. She proposes to answer the question "How does location (specifically, in the U.S., in the 1980s) determine and produce experience and difference as analytical and political categories in feminist 'cross-cultural' work?" ("Feminist Encounters" 31). As the "specifically" indicates, she is attempting to hold on to a materiality of spaces and differences to counter the metaphorization, generalization, and finally erasure of otherness that occurs in Western feminist work on third world women. Western "international" feminism assumes it can move from one place to another and transport its analytic frame unchanged across geographic boundaries. Mohanty wants to preserve the obdurate distance of separate countries to avoid the collapse of cultural locations. "Real land," real geography, in historically, culturally, and politically specific senses, are therefore primary categories for her.

The real of the space she starts with disappears rapidly. In "Feminist Encounters," the transition from a material analytic of space to a more metaphorical one can be read in the flow of the two headings of her subsections: " 'A Place on the Map Is Also a Place in History' " (33) occurs early in the text. While employing space flexibly to name the nonspatial coordinate of history, it also drives toward specificity, the designation of a singular point. This section is succeeded by one entitled, " '. . . it ain't home no more': Rethinking Unity" (38). This title seems to have evaporated the substantiality of place and levered open the closure of the material point represented by "home."

Mohanty cannot maintain the materiality of geographic space precisely because her project is to locate shifting intervals in language rather than to detail the qualities of existing individuals. She uses geography as much as (or more as) a metaphor for the action of discourse than as a referent to existing sites. Language, like topographic space, can be described as a loose, unrealized network *(langue)* organized by relative distances, proximities, connections, and chasms between terms. Its potentials are activated and actualized only in moments of utterance *(parole)*, just as a physical terrain is only realized in moments of traversal. Her project is to map the subjective locations extended by discourses. Mohanty complicates the relations between these discursive positions and the daily existence of real people. For her, to be certain, the three-dimensional form subjects or psyches take does not predate the inscription of subjects by language; nor are these positions fully or permanently embodied by individuals. Like land in geography, subjects in her paradigm are presumed to have a material existence, but her project is to map their surfaces, not to inquire into their depths. Indeed, she evacuates the entire concept of their having an organic "depth," and, like the mappers I will investigate in Chapter Two, obtains an objective distance on, rather than occupying, any of these spaces. She so levels the space of the subject that it becomes impossible to occupy. The critic stands outside the map. She is an oppositional cartographer, and not a sad resident of one of its villages.

Indeed, a later essay, "Cartographies of Struggle," abandons the undecidable subjectivity/objectivity of the terms grounding the earlier essay, the "politics of location" and "experience." Cartography presents itself as an objective measurement of physical data. Mohanty uses this figure to insist on the dissonance of definitions of womanhood across cultural/geographic boundaries. Yet the space she is mapping in this essay is discursive and political, relational in terms of power, so the sites she is recording are hardly immutable. Indeed, that is the argument she is making. The "ground" rapidly mutates into a provisional, flexible fabric: the "world we occupy in the 1990s" is definable "only in *relational* terms" (2), and because relational, necessarily piece-meal and in flux. Hence the ground she begins with is lifted from its moorings and contorted to take on form in discursive, cultural, and subjective realms, in addition to geographical ones. Against Mohanty's intention, the materiality of geography's separations rapidly deterio-rates.

Mohanty's work records her central desire to preserve the materi-ality of separate places at the same time that it releases space as a floating signifier and collapses the distinctions between separable reg-isters of space. In "Feminist Encounters," there is a moment in which the spaces of the subject are both enumerated and strung together, making it to a degree undecidable whether the "counting" which is for Irigaray inseparable from cutting, or the linkage implicit in con-tiguity, is primary.[8] The moment I am referring to appears at the beginning of her essay when she seeks to specify the way she wishes to use the term "the politics of location": "By the politics of location I am referring to the historical, geographical, cultural, psychic and imaginative boundaries which provide the ground for political defi-nition and self-definition for U.S. feminists in 1987" ("Feminist En-counters" 31). Elsewhere in this work and in her other analyses, Mohanty contends that this variety of the spaces of the subject cannot be pinpointed on the basis of a singular origin in one given subject. Yet at this point she presents them in a way that demonstrates their indivisibility, or at the very least their metonymic connectedness. Clearly, to bring the various forms of identity ("historical, geograph-ical, cultural, psychic and imaginative") together will require a more sensitive medium than geography. Against her intention, Mohanty demonstrates that the poststructuralist project to define subjectivity as "subject position" (and no more) is inadequate to explain the com-plexity of postmodern, postcolonial subjects in space.

Rich's essay, like Mohanty's, starts from the solidness of geographic space. She begins: "I am to speak these words in Europe, but I have been searching for them in the United States of America" (210). Rich seeks to limit the power of the primary term—here, "the United States." She couples this monolithic entity with various "other" locations: Nicaragua, England, South Africa. As "the United States of

---

[8]See especially Luce Irigaray, "This Sex Which Is Not One," in *This Sex Which Is Not One*.

America" goes through these successive couplings, its seeping universality is enclosed, bounded on all sides by these other equally present places. Rich attempts to overturn the tendency in a language structured by hierarchized differences for the primary, privileged term to colonize and erase the secondary term. Geographic difference works for her, as for Mohanty, to destroy an originary emphasis upon centrality, a vanity inseparable from ethnocentrism. For each, "geography" provides a metaphoric alternative to writing, replacing (imbalanced) binaries with (equalized) pluralities.

"The United States of America" stands for a national identity and a political attitude, as well as for a locatable place; the essay exposes the correlation of the three. Geography appears explicitly again, when, in relation to Nicaragua, she sees herself as a North American:

> I traveled then to Nicaragua, where . . . under the hills of the Nicaragua–Honduras border, I could physically feel the weight of the United States of North America . . . at my back; I could feel what it means to be part of that raised boot of power, the cold shadow we cast everywhere to the south. (220)

Recognizing her location, she recognizes it as a responsibility—something she cannot set aside. To be thrown into singularity in relation to an "other" means that she will not succumb to the Western temptation to see herself as a disembodied representative of the whole world. At the heart of her project is Rich's attempt to overcome her tendency to generalize her experience as "woman" to "women" everywhere: "And, yes, I need to move outward from the base and center of my feelings, but with a corrective sense that my feelings are not *the* center of feminism" (231). She calls her "struggle for accountability" a struggle to "keep moving" (211). Space allows her to recognize her limitations.

If Mohanty's and Rich's works resemble each other thematically, they differ quite markedly in the spatial format they prefer. Mohanty wants to point out the incompatibility of the spaces I adumbrated at the outset; Rich, by contrast, demonstrates a desire to bind the many forms of subjectivity into a consistent, organic unit. For Rich, geographic placement as an axis of subjectivity flows into national identity as a container of subjectivity; this liquid translation of one parameter of being into the next continues throughout the piece. But just as in

Mohanty's essay the logic of continuity overtook the project of distinction, in Rich's the drive to reconcile spaces shifts at points into a record of their incompatibility. Hence her essay stands as an unexpected example of Mohanty's point: the numerous dimensions of the subject cannot be drawn into a consistent content.

The shift occurs when she is criticizing her own childhood conception of location:

> When I was ten or eleven, early in World War II, a girlfriend and I used to write each other letters addressed like this:
>
> Adrienne Rich
> 14 Edgevale Road
> Baltimore, Maryland
> The United States of America
> The Continent of North America
> The Western Hemisphere
> The Earth
> The Solar System
> The Universe (211–212)

The childish depiction of location puts the self at the center, and lays all surrounding scales of spaces in expanding circles subordinate to and meaningful only in relation to that centrality of self. Rich criticizes this "egotistical" view of space: "You could see your own house as a tiny fleck on an ever-widening landscape, or as the center of it all from which the circles expanded into the infinite unknown. . . . It is that question of feeling at the center that gnaws at me now. At the center of what?" (212). She likewise appears to be criticizing the homogenization of space implicit in this act of centering: all spaces become transparent and consistent as a result of their subordination to the self. She is wise enough to ward this homogenization off, as much as unification is also the central drive of the argument.

And yet, this is one moment in the essay where I believe the nonhomogeneity of the permutations of space she catalogues becomes apparent. While the latter entries might be said to denote only differences of scale in a homogeneous spatial register, the first two are not necessarily mappable locations of the same kind: they open up into territories of meaning that function by a different logic and in different dimensions, into networks of discourse and onto structures of social institutions.

"14 Edgevale Road" denotes a point on a two-dimensional map, certainly, but it is also the label of a *home,* which is on the one hand a three-dimensional structure and on the other a densely signifying marker in ideology. The home separates out "the private" and "the public" and forms a container for the idealized family. Moreover, "14 Edgevale Road" is a signifier caught up in narratives about class: the absence of an apartment number here suggests an air, if not a reality, of privilege. Whether or not the address matches up with the class divisions it suggests, the street name "Edgevale" betrays a whole bourgeois ethos, a desire to live or appear to live like landed gentry in pastoral settings.

The home connects us with a vast interlocking system of cultural and political initiatives. The home is the target for any number of state apparatuses concerning economics, reproduction, political representation, and the like. While today the address carries for individuals of the middle class the banal connotations of a convenience (it ensures we get our mail), in truth the address is a relatively modern invention bearing the trace of rapid urbanization. It is not free of connections to discipline and politics. It tags individuals for easy location by the police; you generally need one to get a job or to receive government support; it is the focal point of the census, which determines the distribution of funds and political representation.[9] It represents a material and social organization of space exceeding the bounds of individual subjects and connecting with the impersonal logic of state power.

Likewise, while "Adrienne Rich" may locate the space of the body, a person's proper name is, even more than the address, a signifier locating the subject in discursive and ideological structures. The proper name propels its bearer into an extracorporeal complex: language, a complex that can be represented in spatial terms, but whose physics

[9] I am certain I have recently read a description of how the address functions within the disciplinary apparatus and serves to locate criminals, but I cannot at the moment find this reference. (As Jane Gallop commented wryly, I "cannot find the address.") Alan Sekula makes some connections along this line in his description of the refinement and standardization of police procedures in "The Body and the Archive," 4–5. On a similar note, Walter Benjamin points out how the long, straight boulevards so dear to the bourgeois conception of the city were actually developed to prevent the building of barricades in Paris and to defeat the revolutionary opposition, in "Paris, Capital of the Nineteenth Century," 159–162.

operates under a very different modality than that of "Baltimore, Maryland." The name "Adrienne" fixes her gender and also suggests nation and ethnicity.

While this spot in Rich's piece can be excavated to demonstrate the incommensurability of the various spaces of the subject, the point of her project remains to join the fragments of the subject together. She does this by using the logic of dimensional containers as her primary spatial emblem. Rich exchanges the graphic, two-dimensional matter of geography and discourse for the three-dimensionality of organic or architectural forms. The flat space laying out semiotic pairs (black/white, straight/lesbian, gentile/Jew, man/woman) mutates, gains depth, grows out to enfold the subject. The boundaries that delimit her positions as a discursive subject turn into walls as she describes how she was born in a hospital "which separated Black and white women in labor and Black and white babies in the nursery, just as it separated Black and white bodies in its morgue" (215). Similarly, capitalist patriarchy stands in as an edifice restricting women and other oppressed peoples from reaching what they need: Rich shifts rapidly on the second page of the essay to a story of a bee trapped in her house, which "bumping, stunning itself against windowpanes and sills" is caught in a place "where it cannot fulfill its own life" (211).

The ultimate destination of her drive toward particularization is another kind of three-dimensional structure, the body: "When I write 'the body,' I see nothing in particular. To write 'my body' plunges me into lived experience, particularity: I see scars, disfigurements, discolorations, damages, losses, as well as what pleases me" (215). She sees it as a space congruent with the other dimensions she has been documenting (e.g., geographic, architectural): "Begin, though, not with a continent or a country or a house, but with the geography closest in—the body" (212). By figuring her body as a closed space, she can align it with the series of other spaces she has enumerated. The body becomes active within the logic of boundaries and the insides and outsides they create.

Whereas Mohanty might locate the subject as the incidental point on a cultural graph, Rich builds it as a three-dimensional volume that the "self" both occupies and is. This figuration of subjectivity allows her to incorporate into her perspective subjective coordinates that fall strictly outside of Mohanty's: the "personal" dimensions of psyche, affect, desire. The location of subjectivity within a three-dimensional architecture allows a much more complex and sensitive registration of emotional reaction than does the simple two-dimensional location of the "subject." In the linguistic plane, she can only be "woman," bearing depersonalized attributes externally applied to her. By seeing subjectivity as a three-dimensional sphere, with an inside and an outside, however, Rich is able to speak of feelings otherwise alien to the political scheme of the subject. "Feelings" come from inside, in response to her "cultural" treatment. The walls separating the terms of binaries in gender and race become the skin surrounding the psyche, upon which are scratched the effects of discursive formations. The three-dimensionality of the psyche allows her to suppose a depth to the subject that is not just the empty *différand* of an antithesis. She can bring into the equation factors thought to predate the subject's involvement in any specific symbolic divide and which continue to resist the impositions of culture: desire, need.

What I find valuable about Rich's essay is the way it takes an "insider's" position, allowing us to incorporate into our theoretical framework personal history and the particular shaping forces of specific kinds of bodies. I criticize Mohanty for doing away with the interiority of the subject, but I do not see Rich negotiating the volume of the subject altogether successfully. Her tendency toward materialism does land her inside the realm of essentialism, I would argue, insofar as "space" acts like "place" for her, existing as origin rather than effect, and causing all the spaces of the subject thereby to coincide. The skin of the body and the skin of the psyche are coterminous and are equated as well with the culturally formulated qualities ascribed to her: woman, white, lesbian, Jew. All of these "containers" are collapsed into one, along the lines of their boundaries.[10] Liz Bondi points out how the more and more precise delimitation and classification of

---

[10]Michael Keith and Steve Pile offer a far harsher reaction than mine to the language of boundaries and containers: "Politically, there is a reactionary vocabulary of both the identity politics of place and a spatialized politics of identity grounded in particular notions of space. It is the rhetoric of origins, of exclusion, of boundary-making, of invasion and succession, or purity and contamination; the glossary of ethnic cleansing." See their "Introduction Part I," to *Place and the Politics of Identity*, 20. While their warning contains much accuracy for the larger discursive world, it seems excessive in relation to theory, and seems too to overlook some of the plasticity of boundaries—a plasticity that occasionally works to undermine fascistic deployments of the rhetoric of containment from within.

identity—Rich's drive to locate herself as a "white, middle-class, lesbian Jew"—can work paradoxically to reinstate the liberal humanist model of individuality: "While [such a practice] challenged misguided assumptions about 'sisterhood' in important and necessary ways, the assertion of multiple identities eclipsed the earlier emphasis on identity as fractured. Reliance upon apparently pre-given categories of class, sexual orientation, race, ethnicity and so on invoked a conception of identity as something to be acknowledged or uncovered rather than constructed, as something fixed rather than changing" (93).

In spite of Rich's attempt to ward it off, there is a continual pull toward the logic of centering as she strives to establish a correspondence among all the differing spatial registers across which her essay roams. The "circles" constituting identity must, if widely scattered, be brought into alignment. Her subjectivity and her body have been "dangerously disconnected" (214) and she wants to link them firmly back together. In order to locate herself, Rich says (as quoted earlier) that she must begin with the geography "closest in—the body" (212), but the interpretation of "closest in" indicates that this body is *already* located and is the margin around the center, her self. As a subject, as a woman, she is already located, in one place. It is not her reclamation of the body as a political territory to fight over that disturbs me, but rather her assumption that her body already and always contained a certain subjectivity, that of "woman." Rich suggests that the limits of identity are fixed, and that we can only fill them properly, rather than play with the limits that have been drawn. This makes it seem (as Mohanty feared) that a consciousness issues quite naturally from one's physical form, as opposed to showing that there can be gaps of greater or lesser magnitude between the body, the psyche, one's political position, one's linguistic position. The body and the psyche may be inexorably pushed together by ideology; to seek consciously to weld them together may therefore be an appropriate political goal. But to see them as naturally linked does reduce the complexity of this interface considerably.[11]

As I see it, each critic runs into some pitfalls in traversing the space

---

[11]Neil Smith and Cindi Katz, in "Grounding Metaphor: Towards a Spatialized Politics," give a consideration of Rich's "politics of location" that covers much the same ground as mine. In the end they find her use of intersubjectivity more destabilizing than I do, and the border negotiations Rich performs that I prefer less so.

of the subject: Rich because she centers space, Mohanty because she objectifies it. However, they maintain the maximum flexibility and specificity of space when they focus on the boundaries constituting particular spaces, and attempt to define the relations between the borders of different spaces. To clarify the promise of the boundary, I'll return briefly to Mohanty's work.

Mohanty's writing features an at-best anxious interest in boundaries. Because she prefers to envision subjectivity as a dispersion of possibilities, she resists the idea of solid boundaries; yet she is also intrigued by the promise that the border as theoretical possibility might hold. I have emphasized the impersonal narrative stance that Mohanty takes, yet "Feminist Encounters," more than other essays I have read by her, has a quite subjective, speculative opening and ending. Toward the close of the piece, she quotes with little interpretation a passage from Alicia Dujovne Ortiz on the boundlessness of the modern city of Buenos Aires: Buenos Aires is not " 'one of those great cities of the world which have such precise boundaries that one can say exactly where they begin and end' "; " 'here geography is merely an abstract line that marks the separation of the earth and sky' " (41). Mohanty then notes:

> In the North America of the 1980s geography seems more and more like "an abstract line that marks the separation of the earth and sky." Even the boundaries between Space and Outer Space are not binding any more. In this expansive continent, how does one locate oneself? And what does location as I have inherited it have to do with self-conscious, strategic location as I choose it now? (41)

Mohanty's capitalization of "Space" makes it seem as if it is something concrete she wants to hold on to, as opposed to the ethereality she has been ascribing it in this passage. The boundary seems to provide a horizon, a promise, even in its evaporation, or because of it. It is as if in turning to the self, to her own self-location and political motivations, and in turning inward to her feelings about the trials that she as a third world woman is put through in the West, the boundary becomes a much more substantial force than it had been throughout the rest of the essay. Possibly too this tenuous enthusiasm is a result of the dissipation of boundaries evident in this passage: the dematerialized boundary provides a utopian hope for those who have found themselves all too compressed by restricting cultural attitudes.

The boundary seems to provide a medium not only for articulating specificity and punctuality, but also for addressing materiality. We suppose that subjects, like all other objects, come to exist only because they have been differentiated, marked by a line from other objects (or subjects). This line can occur in language (in the division between terms); in geography, structured by borders; psychologically, in the separation of the infant from the mother or from reality; and in the political differences between cultural factions. It is across this insubstantial limit that the various parameters of identity seem to meet up: race and gender, for instance, exist upon the same skin, activated simultaneously or separately depending on whom one contacts, that is, upon context. The boundary brings together my edges, as an individual, with the edges of various socially defined groups. It marks too the way these qualities interact with geographic placement: my race and class might have very different meanings depending on which side of the Latin American border I occupy. These possibilities of "thinking through the boundary" are suggested, in "Cartographies of Struggle," by Mohanty's turn to the "borderlands" thematic initiated by Gloria Anzaldúa:

> Consciousness is thus simultaneously singular and plural, located in a theorization of being "on the border." Not any border—but a historically specific one: the U.S./Mexican border. Thus, unlike a Western, postmodernist notion of agency and consciousness which often announces the splintering of the subject, and privileges multiplicity in the abstract, this is a notion of agency born of history and geography. (37)

The important element to maintain would be the temporality of the border: it is not an ontological feature, but an effective, differential one. It holds open a space, but the space it materializes is shifting, temporary, and replaceable. Not immaterial, however: boundary play gives access to substantial interventions in the forms and relations of subjects, but we ought not to assume that the spaces it mediates are somehow empty, or indifferent. As I noted at the outset, boundaries may seem conventional, but their rupture can often reveal a powerful reality about the differences they contain. Negating boundaries established by convention may allow conflicts to be fought out on material, rather than diplomatic and discursive, planes. We test and contest boundaries, cautiously lowering or shifting them, in an attempt to reapportion "spaces," but it is not clear that even such gentle testing can take place without reference to other restrictions—of propriety and ethics.

In many feminist and nonfeminist texts, a lot of excitement accrues around the "inside–outside" dichotomy, as does a lot of uncertainty. It is a utopian limit, but one whose potential and purpose remains unqualified. I am thinking particularly of two examples: Hortense Spillers's " 'An Order of Constancy' " and the introduction to Teresa de Lauretis's *Technologies of Gender.*

In her essay, Spillers is measuring the distance between the eyes that see one and the eye (I) that looks back. Spillers puts perception at the center of the formation of identity: the "most acute aspects of consciousness," she writes, are "to perceive, to be perceived" (244). Spillers talks about the construction of Gwendolyn Brooks's protagonist in *Maud Martha,* and especially about the pitying assumptions that alien and not really sympathetic observers make about her. But just as their gazes pin and consolidate Maud Martha as a certain kind of subject, making her the occupant of a suffocating surface, so Maud Martha looks back, expands her subjectivity beyond those puny boundaries, and makes of herself something quite other. The feminine is an object of others' perceptions, but it is equally a subject who reacts to acts of interpretation and inscription. Her power to look outward, to gaze and to judge in return, is what makes her an estimable person. We have no respect for Paul, her husband, who "doesn't *resist*" (256).

Spillers's model can be used to argue that one cannot take up a wholly externalized view of the subject; to do so is to place one's self in the posture of the ideological apparatus. The whole purpose of fighting over subjective barriers is that they *do* enclose us, they affect as well as effect us, they enable us as much as they may also make us hurt. The sexual, racial, and cultural imperatives of our culture may make us a space of interiority in ways to which we object, but it is from this position that we get the impetus to react to or willfully take up the cultural shape ideology imposes on us.

De Lauretis finds a certain promise too in the idea of being both "inside" and "outside," of sacrificing neither of those perspectives (see esp. p. 10). But she reverses the organic, container–contained relation at work in Spillers's essay: the special province of feminism, she argues, is to be both "inside" and "outside" of the dominant ideology. The "outside" is what corresponds to feminism, something like Dorothy Ardener's "wild zone."[12] The "outside" seems to be more receptive to our physical and psychological needs. But we are also "insiders" of the cultural logic of our time; it is impossible for us to make a subjectivity entirely free of the grasp of the ideology we attack. In some ways, having already claimed the "subjective" as the inside space, I would want to invert de Lauretis's model: that "wild zone," that space of freedom, is inside us, and cultural prescription and constriction is "outside." When we are outside ideology, we are clearly inside something else, and it is either the downfall or promise of de Lauretis's essay that that "something else" seems more real, more natural, closer in correspondence to our desires and our interests as women (in an experiential rather than a biological sense). Promise or downfall: depending on how much one wishes to denaturalize experience to the degree that it is wholly constructed, and not apprehensible except through the lens of an alienating idealogy.

Obviously, I will remain indecisive about this question, because though I expect that all experience is mediated, I still think we feel it, and that some mediations are—not inherently, but situationally— less alienating than others: else why our attraction to feminism? I am tempted, then, to assimilate de Lauretis's model to Spillers's. What I finally find significant about each of these arguments, however, is not the possibility of converting each into a singular pattern that would be "the answer." (In fact, comparing them introduces what will be a common theme of this study: the tendency for the spaces properly "inside" and those properly "outside" to trade places, the crisp outlines of the "monadic" model inevitably undergoing unpredictable mutations.) I want to leave open the psychological space of the subject because I suspect that it is inside in the dark matter of the unconscious, or in its better-lit annex, consciousness, that we begin untying and reweaving the threads of cultural logic, manipulating them to suit our own purposes, so that we can then project our patterns back on

---

[12]Elaine Showalter introduces Ardener's concept in "Feminist Criticism in the Wilderness," 262.

[13]Clearly, I am opposing Judith Butler's argument that concludes *Gender Trouble.* It is not that I disagree with her idea that all change comes from a collision, recombination, and mutation of discourse; I simply disagree with the *site.* She locates it internal to discourse and outside of subjects; I locate it internal to discourse and inside of subjects.

reality.[13] Like Rich, I consider it necessary to view subjectivity as a place where we live, a space we are, on the one hand, compelled to occupy, and, on the other hand, as a space whose interiority affords a place for reaction and response. Hence I am attracted to the possibilities of reforming the spaces of the subject, with working through the boundary as a way of restructuring the organization of society.

Freud locates the functions of perception and consciousness in the surface layer of the cortex and in the quasi-physiological system Perception–Consciousness *(Pcpt.–Cs.)* in *Beyond the Pleasure Principle.* Through these surface layers all stimuli must pass in order to take on a meaning. But "consciousness," in current parlance, has another meaning as well, a political significance deriving from terms such as "consciousness-raising" and "false consciousness." The "psychic skin" and the physical skin that get so confused in Freud's account of consciousness (I will expand on this point in Chapter Three) come together again in our social interactions, as we find ourselves inscribed by discourses on the basis of our visible physical features, and react to the space culture assigns our psychic being. Because culture makes sense of our bodies according to their surface features, I would position political awareness likewise at the surface of subjects, as it seems to me Mohanty does in her speculation about Buenos Aires. Becoming politically conscious might mean becoming conscious of one's own boundaries, feeling the way we live them. Unlike Mohanty, then, I would want to continue figuring political subjectivity as a volume, one with flexible margins, to denote the ways that subjectivity is inhabited by social agents. Becoming politically active might mean bringing the unacknowledged "contents" of subjects up to the surface, where they are open to manipulation.

It is not my intention to claim some "naturality" for the interior. Ideology critique has taught us to see the cultural hand in all of those feelings once deemed "natural," but that does not mean that such capacities of interiority are held any less personally by subjects, including theorists. It is precisely the personalization of such "external" attitudes as patriarchy or feminism that produces such passionate differences between political theorists: compare Phyllis Schlafly and Faye Wattleton. Like Freud, I would see the "interiority" of the subject as a historical achievement, individually, and (to go beyond Freud into Chodorow) culturally. The place and shape and nature of the boundary are never predetermined, or "always-already" there for the subject to assume. Different cultures would surely produce varying contours and sizes for the psychic envelope, with some not holding to a model of "interiority" at all.[14] I would go beyond Freud to Foucault, and suggest that the very basis for a lived inside–out distinction derives from a discursive support.

Even more significantly, the imposition of a boundary between "self" and "space," or (even better) the division between "inside" and "outside" space, participates, according to Freud, in the institution of reality. Tinkering with the boundary might, then, provide a way of changing our reality. The critics I will turn to in later chapters turn to space not only for its descriptive capacities but also because of their starting assumption that a transformation in the discourse defining the space of the subject can effect transformations in the psychic and social realms occupied by the subject. They work with different valences of space and examine their interconnections with the belief that a change in one realm will have a displaced corollary in another.

Both the subject and space have the capacity to be ordered by boundaries; the difference between them seems to be sustained by a fragile boundary. As a result of their common physics and the subtlety of their difference, the two can become intermixed, the difference between them confused. My argument thus far has been not only that critics *deploy* the language of space to concretize their discussions of subjectivity, but also that space infiltrates their depictions of subjectivity to ends that are not always intended or even recognized. The trope of space must be consciously analyzed in order to evaluate its in-flu-ence.

Contemporary theorists seek to break down the inadvertent rigid boundaries associated with the Enlightenment individual, the auton-omous ego, and ontological categories of race and gender, because they consider these hermetic structures the foundation for exclusion and oppression. It might be good to look next at the origin of these "containers" of subjectivity, and at their formation in relation to space. From there, we will investigate how space might form the basis for advancing a responsive and responsible model of the subject, one that neither abandons political realities nor arrests possibilities for change.

---

[14]Possibly one sign of this cultural differential would be the oft-noted cultural variation concerning the appropriate size of "personal space," but this is simply a suggestion.

CHAPTER TWO

Lost in Space

ESTABLISHING THE LIMITS
OF IDENTITY

The Cartesian subject has seemed, to many contemporary theorists, the last (and first) bastion of the current political order. It has been held responsible for the atrocities of imperialism, the subjugation of women, and the psychological illnesses of Western individuals. Lacan objects to its pretense of self-knowledge and self-transparency (particularly in "Of the Subject of Certainty," in *Four Fundamental Concepts*). By denying its location in language, the Cartesian subject cuts itself off from other subjects and from change. Jessica Benjamin critiques its presumption of independence, the way it represses its inevitable relatedness to others by banishing them to preserve its omnipotence. Feminist critics of science, such as Evelyn Fox Keller and Sandra Harding, have pointed to its participation in a structure of knowledge inseparable from domination, arguing that the empirical subject relates to the world only by objectifying it and viewing it at a cold distance. Mary Louis Pratt describes how European travel narratives of the Enlightenment likewise situate the "face of the country" in "sweeping prospects that open up before or, more often, beneath the traveler's eye" ("Scratches on the Face of the Country" 143). Postcolonial critics point out how the imperial subject held the foreign lands and the people in them apart, maintaining them as foreign, "exotic," other, inhuman—separate from the "self," and basically unlike it—or, alternately, incorporated the people and territories

it encountered into its own self-image, obliterating their difference.[1]
Postcolonial critics and feminist critics of the Enlightenment have
catalogued the ways by which the Enlightenment "individual"
founded itself at the expense of others, especially third world populations and women.

A large part of the problem with the Enlightenment individual
derives, it seems, from its spatial form. The "individual" (it has become
a commonplace to point out), is "undivided" within itself, and un-
questionably separate from other subjects and the external environment as a whole. Graphically, the "individual" might be pictured as
a closed circle: its smooth contours ensure its clear division from its
location, as well as assure its internal coherence and consistency.
Descartes's *Meditations on First Philosophy* gesture toward this pictorial
representation of the subject: "I shall now close my eyes, stop up my
ears, withdraw all my senses, I shall even efface from my thinking all
images of corporeal things; or since that can hardly be done, I shall
at least view them as empty and false" (193). Inside the circle of the
rational self all is consistent, cooperating; outside lies a vacuum in
which objects appear within their own bubbles, self-contained and
separate, but largely irrelevant to this autonomous, self-sufficient Ego.
Will, thought, perception might be depicted as rays issuing outward
from this solitary mind to play over the surface of Objects, finally

---

[1]Abdul JanMohamed delineates these opposing colonial strategies well in his "The
Economy of Manichean Allegory: The Function of Racial Difference in Colonialist
Literature": "Colonialist literature is an exploration and a representation of a world
... that has not (yet) been domesticated by European signification. . . . That world is
therefore perceived as uncontrollable, chaotic, unattainable, and ultimately evil. . . .
Faced with an incomprehensible and multifaceted alterity, the European theoretically
has the option of responding to the Other in terms of identity or difference. If he
assumes that he and the Other are essentially identical, then he would tend to ignore
the significant divergences and to judge the Other according to his own cultural
values. If, on the other hand, he assumes that the Other is irremediably different, then
he would have little incentive to adopt the viewpoint of that alterity." (84). If the
imperial subject was a closed circle, it could choose either to draw the unfamiliar into
its own circle or to exclude it—both are unsatisfactory resolutions of the problem of
intercultural encounters. Hence we see that the problem of the (Enlightenment)
individual is not only how it responds to space, but its very spatial form. In "Three
Women's Texts and a Critique of Imperialism," Gayatri Spivak finds the strategy of
forcing the "individualist" model of subjectivity onto third world (women) subjects
particularly damaging, because these subjects may not exhibit the form of subjectivity
Western subjects are thought to possess. Spivak objects to the idea of a dimensional,
interiorized subject on principle.

rejecting them in order to reaffirm its own primacy. Objects that are accepted are pulled in through the walls of the subject and assimilated, thereby restoring the interior once again to blissful homeostasis.[2]

The Cartesian subject, the Enlightenment individual, the autonomous ego of psychoanalysis—all appear to be reducible to this same graphic schema. I use the terms interchangeably to mark out a singular "space of the subject." It's not clear, when contemporary theorists wage war against this model, whether they are speaking of an ideal or of a reality. It has been attacked, on the one hand, as a damaging fiction for the self, and, on the other, as a functional entity responsible for hurting others. It seems safe to call the "monadic" individual a fiction—but a *functional* fiction, one that for all its intangibility, grounds actions and produces effects nonetheless. The fiction seems to be deteriorating of its own accord under the weight of postmodern culture (as Fredric Jameson points out, with reservations); yet as ideal or standard it still carries much power in defining the world and grounding intentional activity. (It is probably a necessary belief for the captains of industry, allowing them to get up, trade stock, and define the fate of the first and third worlds on a daily basis.) It serves, still, to exclude some subjects from pursuits that demand a clear demarcation of self and other, inside and outside: women who mother are too intermixed with "outside" concerns to suit professions that expect isolation and autonomy; the physical envelopes of nonwhite subjects draw too much attention to allow them to occupy positions requiring "neutrality." The world still runs on the idea that "normal" ideal subjects are standardized (though individualized), self-enclosed, self-determining, mobile, and autonomous. Contemporary theorists are both challenging this norm's claim to exhaustively represent subjects and attempting to reconstruct this subject, where it has hardened into reality, to propose more responsive forms of epistemological and social relation.

Even if it never existed as reality, the monadic ideal of subjectivity still has power. Thus it might be interesting to investigate where this

---

[2]Yet the rigorous proof that Descartes needed to arrive at this representation—and the very fact that he felt compelled to produce it—suggest less a certitude than a much deeper and underlying concern about the insubstantiality of the subject. His "proof" might be characterized less as "I think, therefore I am," than as, "I'd better think harder, just to be sure."

ideal came from. While we might find the first insinuations of individualism in Descartes, most critics point to the Enlightenment as the period when the model was first realized—that is, put into practice and widely assumed in discourses. The realization of the Enlightenment individual occurred in tandem with the rise of science and the expansion of imperialism.[3] The subject, imperialism, and science are three divisible areas, but they are inextricably interrelated in one practice: cartography. My argument will be twofold: First, the Enlightenment individual demonstrates a spatial format and projects a particular form for space. The individual and its corresponding form of space arose contemporaneously, with each dialectically reinforcing the other. The "individual" expresses a coherent, consistent, rational space paired with a consistent, stable, organized environment. The relationship between the two is enabled by their separation: clear boundaries ensure the delimitation of inside and outside space, the order of each, and the elevation of the former over the latter. Second, cartography, a science that developed (as a science) in the Renaissance and became standardized during the Enlightenment, is both an expression of the new form of subjectivity and a technology allowing (or causing) the new subjectivity to coalesce. The form for subjectivity, space, and the relation between them inspired by mapping has achieved, I would argue, a kind of popular dominance today—though all three are also beginning, Jameson contends, to "wither away." I will be examining two Renaissance texts of exploration, one by Samuel de Champlain and one by Cabeza de Vaca, to study the roots of cartography's configuration of the subject and space. I will be attempting, too, to offer evidence to support the postcolonial critical contention that the Enlightenment individual is an inherently oppressive and exclusive model for subjectivity, and arguing that these effects are an intrinsic function of that subject's space.

What styles of subjectivity preceded the autonomous ego, the empirical position? It is hard to know, not least because time (and space) limitations prevent me from going beyond the bounds of cartography

---

[3]Of course cartography does not represent the sole "cause" of the Enlightenment subject's spatial form; it is only one practice in an emerging cultural complex. However, it may have had a place at the forefront of this development. R. Hooykaas, in "The Rise of Modern Science," argues that the voyages of exploration were a prime encouragement to the development of "modern science" because of the success they had in applying mechanical instruments to attain knowledge (471).

to earlier spatial practices/subjective positions—either in medieval Europe or in pre-Columbian America. Champlain and de Vaca's texts do suggest that before, or alongside, mapping—both European and Native American—there existed another style of spatial mediation, one based on narrative, that promoted a subject-in-process divided neither from the emotions nor from the omnipresent demands of bodily existence. It is difficult not to draw parallels between this possible subject and the *sujet en procès* or *sujet de différance* of poststructuralism, or the intersubjective subject of American (psychoanalytic) feminism, or the "immanent" intellectual of Foucauldian Marxism. Such romantic comparisons are tempting: after all, if all of these are "oppositional" practices, might there not be similarities among them? But that conclusion is too easy a product of binary thought, a way of ignoring the vast incompatibilities of each of these historical and cultural periods, and the practices developed in them. In Chapter Four, I will be content to discuss the ways poststructuralism has attempted to move knowledge out of the binary paradigm, into the fluid or convoluted differentiations representative of postmodernism.

The spatial format of the Enlightenment individual and the Enlightenment social environment is *bad,* most poststructuralist voices say. Dispensing with cartography (a practice with coincidental, but possibly revealing, ties to that historical period) should then be *good.* If cartography irreparably signifies (and perhaps reproduces?) exploitation, then it should surprise us to "discover," as we will, that the trope and even the practice of cartography are used everywhere in theory today. Fredric Jameson's "Postmodernism, or, the Cultural Logic of Late Capitalism" will provide an example, though surveying language also infiltrates the work of Foucault and other post-Marxist writers (Mohanty among them). Jameson's reflections on postmodernism will reintroduce mapping onto the contemporary critical landscape, and allow us to investigate why current theory has tried so hard to dispose of the Cartesian ego—and why that form of subjectivity may nonetheless persist. Jameson will help to recomplicate the argument by revealing that simply dispensing with established boundaries is no sure formula for utopia—at least, not for everyone.

As I noted in the previous chapter, psychoanalysis (particularly object relations) has held that the subject and space originate from one unified medium that is divided by a subjective boundary. If, as Freud proposed, the structure of the self is achieved through the delimitation of an external environment, then the form for the environment that the self produces will recursively dictate the shape of the self. Richard Helgerson's work suggests that the symbiotic shaping of environment and self occurs not only in the psychological developmental process that forms each individual, but also in the cultural and historical processes that went into shaping *the* individual, or any other form that subjectivity has historically taken. In "The Land Speaks: Cartography, Chorography, and Subversion in Renaissance England," Helgerson examines the relation between mapping and the subject and the historical relationship of both to the centralized power of the sovereign: "One hears much of the Renaissance discovery of the self and much too of the Elizabethan discovery of England. . . . Not only does the emergence of the land parallel the emergence of the individual authorial self, the one enforces and depends on the other" (64). The land and the individual came into existence at the same time as a result of their difference from a third term: the queen.

Edmundo O'Gorman similarly remarks that the modern concept of the "sovereign self" depended upon the development of the Western spatial imagination. Before the ideo-geographic developments of the Renaissance, Eurasia was thought to be the sole land mass, surrounded by water. The realization that the lands newly found by Columbus (and imagined by him to certainly be part of Eurasia) were actually a *different* continent collapsed the space of Europe and initiated the new astronomical sciences that would reconceptualize the globe as a single small gear in the machinery of a universe no longer necessarily controlled by God. This in turn made "man" able to conceive of himself as an independent actor, author of his peregrinations, master of his world. It was the first step in separating "man" from his environment, the first turn of a spiraling trajectory that would eventually—first in his mind, then in his body—fling him off the globe. The reconception of the world that allowed the newfound Americas to be conceived as a separate continent may have been a key step on the path to the modern ideology of the individual.

Mapping, then, comes onto the scene both to reflect and to reinforce a new way of conceiving both the subject and space. What kind of space, what kind of subject, does mapping (per)form? It organizes the landscape in such a way that some aspects of "reality" are privileged while others are silenced (Harley, "Silences" 66).[4] Cartography selectively emphasizes boundaries over sites. Harley argues that such an emphasis indicates the primacy in European mapping of *ownership* ("Victims" 32). One could transfer this insight into the realm of the subject by pointing out the emphasis upon "propriety" and "ownness" in the "one-ness" of the Enlightenment individual—as well as this subject's imbrication in the developing social form of capitalism.

At the same time, boundaries will not become a significant—and troublesome—quality of the subject until at least the Romantics. During the expansion of cartography, boundaries for the psychic and somatic individual tended more to be asserted than investigated. Leibniz provides a good example in his philosophization of "monadalogy," in 1714. All objects that are indivisible, in spite of being internally differentiated, including people, fall under the heading of "monads." According to Leibniz, "Monads have no windows, by which anything could come in or go out. Accidents cannot become detached, or wander about outside substances. . . . Thus neither substance nor accident can enter a monad from without" (179). Leibniz does some fancy philosophical footwork to explain how bodies connect to souls, how they can change over time, and how they relate to the universe outside themselves. But he maintains that their boundaries are constant, if flexible: "The organic bodies of nature are never produced from a chaos or putrefaction, but always from seeds, wherein there was certainly some *preformation* . . . [from this] we conclude not only that the organic body was already present before conception, but also that there was a soul in this body" (191, italics in original). The boundaries of the subject, like the boundaries beginning to crisscross

---

[4]Cultural geography, a branch of geography influenced by political—particularly Marxist—discourses and French poststructuralist theory, seeks to demonstrate that the organization of space, like any other aspect of the real, is conventional, to some degree arbitrary, and indisputably culturally specific. I thank J. B. Harley for patiently directing me through this important field of study, still little known in many English departments, and for the trenchant analyses his essays provide. A good introduction to cultural geography can be found in an anthology edited by Derek Gregory and Rex Walford, *Horizons in Human Geography*. Chapter Two of Derek Gregory's *Geographical Imaginations* provides a useful history of the influence of poststructural theory in the genesis of social geography.

the land at this time, were just beginning to be formalized. But in either case, the conventionality of these boundaries did not induce doubt about their validity or rightness.

Another disposition of post-Medieval conceptions of space was standardization. Harley demonstrates the tendency of early American cartographers "to obliterate the uniqueness of the American landscape in favour of a stereotype" reflecting a European sense of the natural world ("Silences" 68); their maps thereby helped promote the new lands for colonization. (The maps included in the French text of Champlain's journey, to take one example, feature uniformly shaped and spaced trees and hills and a smattering of deer, bear, beavers, fish, and armed or naked *"sauvages"* in an otherwise blank territory.) This conventional kind of representation seems to ignore the actual features of the territory. According to Harley,

> Behind the facade of a few standard signs on these [early modern European] atlases, the outline of one town looks much the same as that of the next; the villages are more nearly identical and are arranged in a neat taxonomic hierarchy; woodland is aggregated into a few types; even rivers and streams become reduced into a mere token of reality; objects outside the surveyor's classification of "reality" are excluded. . . . The net result was that the cartographic landscapes of Europe became more generalized, more abstract, and less differenti- ated in the mode of their representation. Their silences are those of the unique. ("Silences" 65)

This conception of space once again parallels the form increasingly being extended to the individual. One of the primary assumptions of Enlightenment humanism concerned the universal quality of human- ity: one interchangeable, generalizable model for subjects appeared to exhaust the possibilities of human Being. This conception of "Man" displays serious limitations, excluding as it does any number of "sub- jects" who deviate from its norm (e.g., women, African American slaves, colonized peoples). Standardized "Man," like mapping iconog- raphy, applied its own culturally specific standards as if they were indeed universal to the end that actual otherness was erased. Subjects, like places, were homogenized in favor of the generic, such that social policy based on humanism has proven to be insensitive to the varying needs of "different" subjects. Harley details the same effect in relation to space: "Space becomes more important than place: if places look

alike they can be treated alike" ("Silences" 66). In speaking of the
Enlightenment conception of the individual, it would be possible to
paraphrase Harley's statement above: its silences were those of the
different.

Changes in the aesthetic appearance of maps testified to the growing
authority of scientific discourse, which would terminate in an erasure
from the map of all signs of the immediately subjective. The "central
bastions" of European mapping from the 17th century onward "were
measurement and standardization and beyond there was a 'not
cartography' land where lurked an army of inaccurate, heretical, subjective, valuative, and ideologically distorted images" (Harley,
"Deconstructing" 4–5). Internal to and enabling mapping lives a
dichotomy between "fact" and "nonfact"; according to its logic, any
perception achieved outside its parameters must necessarily be "untrue." In mapping, as in the conception of individuality, objectivity
comes to the fore as the sole arbiter of truth and reality. Logic and
reason increasingly dominate the scheme of the mind, acting as the
orienting principles of personhood. In both realms, idiosyncrasy and
emotionality, physicality and specificity, are increasingly marginalized.

Though based on a claim of objectivity, mapping cannot encompass
all aspects of spatial experience, and it operates best in a situation
where its own grounding principles remain veiled. The cultural and
subjective location of mapping are elided, much as are the problematics
of subjectivity for the Enlightenment individual. Each tends to project
outward, to let the beam of attention play across the surrounding
world, rather than turning its cognition on itself. The Western subject
during the Enlightenment tended to define itself by cataloguing *others*
(e.g., women, natives, criminals, the insane) which it opposed because
it did not require definition. Humanism constructs paradigms for
deviant subjectivity from which it absents itself. Likewise, the primary
silence in mapping, Harley stresses, is that of the subject performing
the mapping. Scientific cartography, he writes, serves to "dehumanize
the landscape. Such maps convey knowledge where the subject is kept
at bay. . . . Thus, with the progress of scientific mapping, space became
all too easily a socially empty commodity, a geometrical landscape of
cold, non-human facts" ("Silences" 66).[5] Mapping reintroduces the

[5]Sandra Harding's *The Science Question in Feminism* is much concerned with this
phenomenon in contemporary science.

subject through the back door in the form of unrecognized cultural biases, presupposing a certain *ideal* subject.

The space that mapping propagates is an immutable space organized by invariable boundaries, an atemporal, objective, transparent space. Not coincidentally, the same physical qualities characterize the kind of subjectivity that we would name, variously, Cartesian monadism, Enlightenment individualism, or autonomous egoism. But the relationship is not only metaphoric, one of comparability; it is also metonymic—one of contiguity. The similarity of mapped space and the mapping subject stems from the way the boundary between them is patterned as a constant barricade enforcing the difference between the two sites, preventing admixture or the diffusion of either entity. Cartography institutes a particular kind of boundary between the subject and space, but is also itself an interface, mediating the relationship between space and the subject and constructing each in its own particularly ossified way.

Samuel de Champlain, in a number of trips from 1609 to 1618, supported by a host of soldiers, missionaries, and laborers, explored the St. Lawrence Gulf area of what is now known as the Canadian Maritime Provinces and Quebec. Cabeza de Vaca followed a circuitous course through the southeast quadrant of the North American continent on an unplanned and unwilled journey lasting from 1527 to 1537. His party intended to carry out a brief reconnaissance, but through a series of disasters they lost their ships, their commander, their arms, their clothing, and their way. The overland journey from what is now Florida to New Mexico to return to the Spanish dominion finally reduced the original party of 300 to 4.

These two narrators are bounded the same way geographically and historically. Behind them, Europe; before them, the utterly unknown. Behind them, land stabilized by representation; before them, an unformed and unsignifying universe. Their texts both are and are not documents on the same order as maps. Graphic representations of geography conceal the temporal dimension of the journey through space, summarizing what was encountered only bit by bit into one frame that makes knowledge appear total and transparent. The two texts balance across what now seem to be two opposed subjective structures: the affective, personalized narrative subject in process, and the arrested, reinforced, omniscient subject of "objectivity." The narrators maintain the hermetic self of graphic cartography always just ahead as their goal, making the "ego" of these texts the ideal object projected by the far more tenuous "subject" (Lacan describes subjectivity in these terms).[6] Both for the subjects they are and the world they encounter, the explorers maintain an ideal of stable, rationalized space while actually occupying a space that is chaotic and seemingly mobile. While Champlain and de Vaca chase after their ideal of land and of subjecthood, their historical position and the generic constraints of their texts prevent them from fully occupying such stabilized spaces.

Our customary bias is to assume that mapping comes to an object—space—that is already formed and needs only to be perceived. Edmundo O'Gorman argues that in examining the history of exploration, we need to "focus historical events in the light of an ontological perspective, i.e., as a process producing historical entities instead of a process, as is usually assumed, which takes for granted the being of such entities as something logically prior to it" (4).[7] Too often in reading the narratives of discovery, we forget the gradualness of the explorers' coming-to-be-located, the long time they spent in an as-yet-unorganized environment. Thus when we reread the literature of exploration we need to read it as a process of *creating* the geography. Likewise, we need to analyze these texts not as accounts of the journeys of individuals, but as stopping points on the journey to *the* Enlightenment individual.

Editors and critics of texts like de Vaca's and Champlain's often

---

[6]Chandra Mukerji's work suggests that much of the earliest geographical knowledge (i.e., from Columbus's voyages) was originally preserved and communicated in narrative or epistolary—not graphic—form, and many pictographic maps were generated from research done in writing (cf. "A New World-Picture" 95, 101). I maintain that narrative and pictorial maps share a common preconception of what knowledge is and how the subject is to obtain it; the same relation holds between early and contemporary maps, regardless of how "artistic," even fanciful, maps from the Renaissance now appear. Narrative and early graphic maps do differ from contemporary scientific cartography, however, in their capacity to display the gaps in the apparatus of mapping.

[7]Evelyn Page makes an even larger argument: the very concept of American literature, she contends, erases the true history of exploration, presupposing a distinct geographical and nationally bounded territory, when it was precisely this place that the literature of conquest created (7).

circumvent such a recognition. At the end of Chapter Forty-four of Cabeza de Vaca's text, *Adventures in the Unknown Interior of America,* an interesting narrative event occurs. The editor, Cyclone Covey, asserts that

> Cabeza de Vaca, admittedly confused in his recollections in this section, is resummarizing the segment of the trip he has already traced. In both editions of his narrative, in fact, this reminiscence comes after the crossing of the mountains, but is here transposed back to its proper place. (107–108)

In other words, the editor, standing on the now-mapped firmament, knows the "proper" place of the episodes. Covey's correction implies that the land was "out there" for de Vaca to measure, when in fact it was his measurement, however faulty and partial, that *created* the stable surface that the present editor can now occupy with such confidence. A similar interpolation in Champlain's text would be this footnote, after Champlain's sentence, "The 17th of the month I took the altitude, and found the latitude 45° 25′ ": "Really 44° 25′ " (50). What difference could such a discrepancy make to the modern reader (taking for granted that this reader is not seeking topographical fact)? Provided with such information, the reader is offered an illusion of total knowledge, a formalized space and fortified subject position, that the texts themselves could only strive to achieve.[8]

[8]In order to interpret the writings of the early explorers at all, literary critics have often felt compelled to interpret them as literature, foregrounding their narrative and poetic aspects at the expense of the cartographic material involved. But Evelyn Page notes that the anecdotal interludes of primary interest to scholars today were originally the secondary or supplementary part of the texts, whose main purpose was to record exploration (16). The blend of narrative and topological detail in these accounts springs in part from the character of the authors, who were not "artists" but sailors and soldiers. These accounts quite literally "account" the cost of these voyages to their patrons. Further, "literary" and "scientific" discourse had not yet diverged. Mukerji explains that it was not until the 17th century that narrative was expunged from professional sailors' records, and technical information disappeared from popular accounts, as "science" came into its own as a distinct practice (105). The fact that very little literary criticism of this genre exists suggests that the texts, like maps, are considered historical or scientific artifacts of greater or lesser veracity, rather than texts whose stylistics and conventions need to be read. Critics decide to read these writings as either "science" or "art," and construct the narrating subject accordingly. Either way, they have reduced the complexity of the writings considerably; these works might best be read as loci where a number of subject positions or structures intersect, or have yet to be fully differentiated.

The externalization and control of space the texts seek to propagate goes hand in hand with their attempt to formulate a safely encapsulated subject; and cartography seems the ideal method for establishing both. The exploratory accounts of Champlain and de Vaca swell with cartographic details. I select the following passage from *The Voyages of Samuel de Champlain, 1604–1618* nearly at random. These descriptions of "Long Island" appear in two succeeding paragraphs:

> Being distant quarter of a league from the coast, we went to an island called Long Island, lying north-north-east and south-south-west, which makes an opening into the great Bay Francoise, so named by Sieur de Monts.
> This island is six leagues long, and nearly a league broad in some places, in others only a quarter of a league. It is covered with an abundance of wood, such as pines and birch. (30)

Of these sentences, only one dwells upon sensible, physical characteristics of the island (its trees). There is almost no paragraph in the text that does not exhibit the same qualities: a listing of features with little interpretation or judgment (beyond whether the land is favorable or not to commerce and sustenance); little affect; great amounts of objective and instrumental (in both senses) information. The land is externalized from the subject and held at a distance; the subject is expelled from the landscape and becomes alien to it. Though relation there must be for perception to occur, Champlain describes what he sees as much as possible as if he were not there, as if no one were there, as if the island he details exists wholly outside any act of human perception. At the inception of his narrative, then, Champlain is able to maintain the ideal of an encapsulated, independent space for his subjectivity that will be the hallmark of Cartesian monadism, where the relationship between subject and environment is attenuated, with the second term evacuated to a high degree to ensure the uncontaminated primacy of the self.

The mapper is an alien in another way too: he is, and encodes himself in his text as, a foreigner. Mapping itself indicates that the subject is not a native to the land—otherwise, the activity would be unnecessary. Who needs maps to get around his own house? Champlain describes the foreign land in order to display it to an absent audience, as if he were displaying a mysterious imported object before the principals of the court. Their absence is inscribed within the text and enables it, and it is with this position of absence that Champlain identifies.

Nearly all the explorers' descriptions are generic, telling only whether a spot is barren or fair—and they called "barren" many locations magnificent (to the modern eye) with woods, mountains, and streams. Their insensitivity to their surroundings results, Page suggests, from their "empirical . . . school of nature" (195). Romanticism, which would have given the explorers the lens to see in Nature an inherent meaning or beauty (no less an ideological project), was still several centuries in the future. The interpenetration of subject and environment that marks romanticism's foregrounding of Nature does not appear here: the interpretive frame is one of objective measurement motivated by the prospects of profit. Champlain identifies with Capital, and to the degree that he does so, he positions himself as European, inevitably alien to the New World.

But his vision does not even find a home in Europe. It is suspended above the globe, up in the heavens someplace where he can see the whole world, view the network of longitude and latitude, and place topological features within its matrix. The cartographer removes himself from the actual landscape, externalizing the surroundings from his body so that he can reapprehend them through a conventionalized system of representation in which all topographies, however various, can be indiscriminately substituted. Mapping separates the subject conceptually from his actual location. While any representation could be said to do the same, this separation is mapping's *purpose,* and it is judged successful only to the degree that it does so.

The texts carry a disjuncture between passages locating the subject as a mapper and those "narrative" passages that reveal a different kind of subject—and a different sense of space. Part of the function of mapping, it would seem, is to ensure that the relationship between knower and known remains unidirectional. The mapper should be able to "master" his environment, occupy a secure and superior position in relation to it, without it affecting him in return. This stance of superiority crumbles when the explorers' cartographic aptitude deteriorates. When they are lost, a different kind of subject emerges, a diffracted, porous self fused with a chaotic and mobile environment.

To actually be *in* the surroundings, incapable of separating one's self from them in a larger objective representation, is, for the explorers, to be lost. "Being lost" may seem antithetical to the literature of exploration, but it is the underlying truth of these texts and is one of their most significant practical and affective elements. Because Champlain and de Vaca are foreigners, their "being lost" signifies the real situation of the explorers in the New World. Even when, according to their calculations (upon which they depended in spite of the fact that they were frequently misled), the explorers knew where they were, operating in the New World prevented them from assuming the position of mastery they possessed in their homelands, where their travels carried them (one would assume) to destinations known in advance across already ordered spaces.

The environment that the explorers experienced may have had little to do with the fixed space we are accustomed to occupying now. The following passage, in which Champlain describes the misadventures of his ship in ice and fog during his voyage of 1611, may better communicate what the experience of America was like in the beginning. The land he faced itself appeared to have some of the fluid characteristics of this world of water, floating ice, obscuring fog, and darkness. The account lasts five pages (an unusual length in this context), but a few lines will suffice to capture its tenor:

> The most self-possessed would have lost all judgement in such a juncture; even the greatest navigator in the world. What alarmed us still more [than the ice] was the short distance we could see, and the fact that the night was coming on, and that we could not make a shift of a quarter of a league without finding a bank or some ice. (199–200)

The land Champlain faces appears chaotic and unstable, moving according to its own unpredictable logic. Champlain's vision and his consciousness are increasingly compressed; the land's attributes are magnified until where he *is* seems the whole world. The explorer is helplessly *located*, but since he does not know where he is, the environment, rather than being a stable field he moves across, appears to be reorganizing around him. The Native American environment was in real ways dynamic. There were few permanent settlements, spots that could be mapped in the manner of European cities; there were no stable boundaries to cross or identifiable territories to locate. Locations were fluid, defined by contact along the edges of moving groups of peoples.

Champlain observes frequently, "If the land were cleared up, grain would flourish excellently" (41). The phrase "cleared up," though an accident of translation, faithfully conveys his tendency to see the land as a problem, a thing awaiting order. (The phrase in the original French text is *"estõiet déffrichées"* [33].) The American environment will not conform to an already established plan, one with fixed sites connected by well-beaten paths, as in Europe. The landscape travels along the pathways of the senses and penetrates the body, thereby endangering the hermetically sealed subject. The environment of the explorers resembles that disordered, fragmented world of the pre-Oedipal phrase described by Freud in relation to the "oceanic feeling," but their location in it does not lead to a kind of infantile pleasure. It leads to anxiety.

For Champlain, whose mission was successful overall, such rendings of the veil of mastery are rare. His narrative retains at least the *hope* of mastering his environment. De Vaca has given up even that possibility. He diagnoses the European's position in the American landscape much more lucidly:

> By the time we reached my previous campsite, it was painfully clear to all that we were unprepared to go further. Had we been prepared, we still did not know where to go. . . . I will not prolong this unpleasantness; but you can imagine what it would be like in a strange, remote land, destitute of means either to remain or get out. (44)

It is interesting that de Vaca sees difficulty in *remaining* as well as in *departing*. Cartographic orientation would seem perfectly adequate for getting out of a place (indeed, that is its main function), but we rarely realize how useless it is for staying put. Because he cannot separate himself from the environment, it takes on an undifferentiated quality in which such measures as "here" and "there," "inside" and "outside," and the distinctions between them cease to exist—cease, that is, to make any difference as orienting principles. In the absence of a cognitive map, movement has no relevance.

The reason the explorers are so frequently "lost" is that they are going somewhere, but are unable to integrate conceptual space and real space, and even their conceptual space is fragmentary (the same structure describes our experiences of being lost today). Being "lost" not only describes the subject *in* space; it describes the subject *as* space. The elevation of the subject over its surrounding space collapses; the minute vacuum assuring their separation disintegrates, likewise de-composing the pure compartmentalization of the subject. "Being lost" becomes something like a crisis of differentiation, a dysfunction of the logic ensuring ordered space. I would extend this observation to propose that the Enlightenment subject's maintenance of the differ-ence between interiority and exteriority enables a stationary organi-zation for the external world—both physical and social. Additionally, I would suggest that one of the prime characteristics of the "individ-ual" is this teleological orientation—continuity in time—rather than conscious structuration in space. Maintaining a stable space outside allows a subject to maintain his form even as he moves through it. Upsetting the distinctions of near and far, inside and outside, brings into question what is proper to the subject.

In spite of his long cohabitation with the Indians, de Vaca remains "lost" throughout his journey (though at some times he is more so than at others) because he is continually diverted from his straight path toward the Spanish colony. He feels "lost" even when the Indians he accompanies know exactly where they are. He is lost because his concept of orientation relies on getting out of a place, separating himself from it, rather than becoming integrally involved with it. He is consistently frustrated by the seeming wandering of his hosts:

> As we were about to get on next morning, the local villagers all wanted to take us to friends of theirs who lived at the top of the ridge. . . . But it was out of our way and we decided to continue our course on the same trail. . . . When the Indians saw our determination to keep to this course, they warned us that we would find nobody, nor prickly pears or anything else to eat. (104–105)

There is a lasting conflict between the intentions of the Indians, which appeared to be based on easily revised narratives tending toward immediate goals, and that of de Vaca, who wishes to travel in one direction, on a straight line.

De Vaca frequently receives invitations to "become" an "Indian." But the explorers are incapable, ideologically as well as practically, of doing so. Colonization was from the start arranged hierarchically, not as a meeting between equals; the explorers wish to influence and possess the world they meet, but take great pains to be sure that it will not substantially inform them in return. They evacuate the others they meet, keeping their own subject position in the form of the already formulated, complete monad. They want to get *away* from America (and its inhabitants), to maintain its position "outside" themselves, and not change dramatically as a result of their relationship with it. Their contact with it remains marked by distance, a series of separations set up to ensure the continuity of self.

Dissonance between the European and the Native American methods of environmental negotiation is a source of political as well as dramatic tension throughout the text. While scholars today may consider mapping's involvement with imperialism coincidental, the relation between cartography, capitalism, and authority, the admixture of religion and rapacity, was hardly unconscious to the explorers. In recommending himself to the queen regent of France in a prefatory letter to his accounts, Champlain declares awareness of the role that mapping must play in conversion and commerce:

> Of all the most useful and excellent arts, that of navigation has always seemed to me to occupy the first place. . . . By this art we obtain knowledge of different countries, regions, and realms. By it we attract and bring to our own land all kinds of riches, by it the idolatry of paganism is overthrown and Christianity proclaimed throughout all the regions of the earth. (17)

While it seems obvious that mapping would need to precede colonization, here Champlain seems to be making a larger claim: mapping is directly instrumental in making the new land a commodity and subduing the native people. The form cartography gives to contact between cultures and the subject position it institutes somehow interlock with its imperialist uses.

Maps constitute geography according to their own cultural matrix. The maps the explorers made, though created in response to the features of the New World, transpose into the new space the logic of Europe. Because the Native Americans did not map according to European standards, Europeans believed that they did not have any necessary relationship to the land. Native American geographic practices could not be recognized by the Europeans as equal manifestations of ownership; in fact, they could not be recognized at all. Native American practices of orientation, like their customs of habitation and dress, did not amount, in the European view, to a "recognizable social order." As Powell states, most Native American individuals and tribes depended more upon rules of customary use than upon nominal ownership (87). In describing a people called the Etechemins, Champlain declares: "They are a people who have no fixed abode. . . . For they spend the winter now in one place and now in another, according as they find the best hunting." (48). Champlain admonishes them not only for their profligacy and lack of foresight, but also for their lack of a fixed address. Frederick Turner writes, "Indeed, the primitives' harmonious and precise knowledge of their habitats came in the process of the 'Europeanization' of the globe to be the very mark of the primitive itself" (11). Thus their lands could be taken from them by Europeans who suffered no guilt, even if the seizure entailed bloodshed.

But as Todorov demonstrates, even this formulation—that mapping preceded the bloodshed—conceals the inherent power of mapping: "Perhaps there is a simplistic utopianism in thus reducing matters to the use of violence, especially since violence, as we know, can take forms that are not really subtler but less obvious." (181). The relation of power to knowledge in conquest is not, Todorov argues, contingent but constitutive (181). Mapping embodies colonization: materializing the land according to a European logic erases the order it might formerly have possessed, converting it into European land. The colonists *created* the land as they explored it, coming to New Worlds as if they were unoccupied—blank—virgin. Their naming literally transformed the land into one that America's original inhabitants, occupying a different world, could not fit.

The European explorers attempted to maintain the environment on the "outside" in order to preserve their mastery of it. As de Vaca's testimonies relate, the Europeans also needed to maintain the Native Americans as external in order to reinforce their own subjectivity. By attributing inferiority to the Native American peoples and their spatial practices, these texts functioned to concretize individualism and ensure the Native Americans' exclusion from it. The solid lines that cartography draws between the subject and the land also reinforced the European subject's white Western identity.

Cartography helped advance and consummate the primacy of boundaries. It demarcated territories within occupied lands to establish legal ownership, and, as it projected overseas, it functioned to denote the separation between Europe and those spaces designated "other." In sociological terms, moreover, it distinguished "self" from "other": in the American instance, cartography was the measure between human and nonhuman, civilized and savage. My argument has been that mapping both advances and symptomatizes a larger cultural order premised on cleanly distinguishing between entities in the natural environment, the psychic environment, and finally, the social environment.

※✦☲✦※

In the last few decades, the Enlightenment subject mapping helped fortify has come under fire, not only in poststructural criticism, but also, Fredric Jameson argues, in its everyday attempt to negotiate external (cultural and physical) space.

Jameson's essay "Postmodernism, or, the Cultural Logic of Late Capitalism" describes postmodernism as a scene where the matrix of space has abolished categories of time, but space itself has exceeded its traditional organization. He sees postmodernism as an expanding chaos of stimuli unordered by a selective grid of meaning, between whose elements there are no hierarchies, and within which distance and difference are increasingly collapsed. Jameson pairs the new unmanageability of built space with the slipping away of an ordered, obvious direction for intellectual and political practice. (Here he is not so far from the explorers, as in either situation the whole purpose of representing space is to determine a way to *act*.) Jameson's technique to recolonize this fragmented and fluid environment is, like the explorers', to import maps.

Jameson's description is surprisingly familiar, in the light of those made by Champlain and de Vaca. The disorientation contemporary space imposes is exemplified for Jameson in postmodern architecture. His description of late capitalist space reaches its intentionally dizzying culmination in a description of the Bonaventure Hotel in Los Angeles:

> I am more at a loss when it comes to conveying the thing itself, the experience of space you undergo. . . . I am tempted to say that such space makes it impossible for us to use the language of volume or volumes any longer. . . . You are in this hyperspace up to your eyes and body. . . . It has been obvious, since the very opening of the hotel in 1977, that nobody could ever find any of these stores. . . . So I come finally to my principal point here, that this latest mutation in space—postmodern hyperspace—has finally succeeded in transcending the capacities of the individual human body to locate itself, to organize its immediate surroundings perceptually, and cognitively to map its position in a mappable external world. (82–83)

"Postmodernism" reproduces on a higher level the anxieties and assumptions concerning space, place, and orientation that mark the texts of Champlain and de Vaca. Its thrust is hardly conservative, as Jameson carves out for himself an authorial position both strongly Marxist and productively engaged with postmodern culture. (I should express here my admiration for this essay, which is enormously productive in spite of it shortcomings—or possibly, productive precisely *where* it is problematic.) Yet not unlike Champlain, Jameson tends to see the postmodern landscape as a problem, one that needs clearing up. His usual forms of orientation are disabled; he finds no clearly marked or familiar reference points in the way he is accustomed to thinking of them. This space, like that of the explorers, erases the meaningful discriminations of "here" and "there," "before" and "after," that allow the plotting of a trajectory. Given the way he has framed the "problem" of the postmodern landscape, Jameson's solution—"the need for maps"—arrives as a great relief. It is his contention that postmodern space is a "problem" that I will be investigating: A problem for whom? And why?

The power of Jameson's assertions comes from his supposition that anyone who entered this space would experience it the same way. But, like the Renaissance explorers, he is issuing onto an unfamiliar landscape and seeking to treat it like a familiar one. The implied "I" here or the frequently used "we" is not the native entering a transformed world, as he would have us believe, but a foreigner exploring new and unfamiliar terrain. Surely if he visited this site frequently, as a shop girl or maintenance man, he would gain a working knowledge of it, as much as he might also come to detest it. As Doreen Massey indicates, "The ways in which people are inserted into and placed within this 'time–space compression' are highly complicated and extremely varied [and very much derived from their sex, race, ethnicity, nation, and economic means]. . . . Moreover, recognition of this complexity raises the important issue of *which* condition of postmodernity are we talking about—whose . . . ?" (62).[9] Like the

---

[9]What Jameson calls "postmodern hyperspace," David Harvey, a cultural geographer, calls "time–space compression." Harvey's *The Condition of Postmodernity* could have provided a similar ground for making my argument, but I selected Jameson's because of its greater influence in the broader field of cultural studies and literary theory, as well as for its greater poetry and personalism.

colonialists, his very ability to encounter this foreign space results from the economic and cultural privilege that allows him to travel to unfamiliar landscapes—for them, as agents of Capital; for him, as its heir. He is a tourist.

Moreover, Jameson has alienated *himself* from this environment in some ways by being an academic Marxist, who wishes to stand outside the edifices of a capitalist world structure, in opposition to it. His method of cultural orientation, classical Marxism, demands that he, like the earlier mappers (both are located by the predicates of science), needs to be at an objective distance from the phenomena he seeks to analyze. The disorientation he attributes to a change in the environment might be charged instead to his navigational method: note that he defines the world as an "external mappable" world. What we see when we read Jameson's essay is the deterioration of the space established by the explorers and the crisis of the subject associated with it, the monadic "space-capsule."

It could be observed that Jameson identifies in the postmodern landscape a *derealization* of space, its plasticity, its tendency to become an infinite semiosis with no resting point, its evacuation of a secure external referent. The intrusion of unevaluative, homogeneous, "undialectical" space[10] exhausts traditional modes of determining "difference," especially hierarchy. He censures theories of difference that "stress disjunction" to the point that structures "fall apart into random and inert passivity," becoming a "set of elements which entertain purely external separations from one another" (75). He seems to want a *substantial,* essential, difference—a volume—not just a structure that is an effect of an arbitrary boundary. His essay strains to reinstate boundaries that are rapidly becoming far too ephemeral; one of the most representative features of postmodernism, as Jameson describes it, is its erasure of lines that had previously kept separate phenomena and objects apart. Postmodernism cannibalizes everything into its own dizzyingly productive circuit: "Everything in our social life . . . —to the very structure of the psyche itself—can be said to have become 'cultural' in some original and as yet untheorized sense" (87). Jameson does not take this observation to its logical conclusion—that the boundary always was arbitrary and "cultural." Hence he disposes of

[10]I am borrowing this phrase from Foucault's "Questions on Geography" in *Power/Knowledge.*

the very possibility that has caused poststructuralism to focus on the boundary—that the world can be reenvisioned and revised via human negotiation.

In this essay, boundaries of all kinds are on the one hand highly emphasized and deemed necessary, but on the other hand problematized and metaphorized. In Jameson's postmodernism, all coalesces: the inside becomes indistinguishable from the outside, flatness surpasses depth, the surface melts and takes on a luminous presence with a life separate from the object itself. From the great, contorted, concentric loops of the "sealed membrane" of Edvard Munch's homunculus in *The Scream* (62–63), to the vacuity of present-day film personalities (68), to the glossy polyester skin of Duane Hanson's "dead and flesh-colored simulacra" displacing reality with "stereoscopic illusion" ("But is this now a terrifying or exhilarating experience?") (76–77), to the repulsive glass skin of the Bonaventure Hotel, reminiscent of a cop's mirrored sunglasses in its inhuman aggressivity (82), surfaces and borders are put into a derealizing play reminiscent less of the frontier-bursting transgression of laughter than the out-of-control feeling of a carnival ride: we are swept up in a stomach-turning confusion of surface and content, illusion and reality, that isn't much fun, that nauseates and defeats rather than welcomes and pleases.

The postmodern subject, like the postmodern landscape it occupies in a relation of mutual reinforcement, has lost its traditional form of closed interiority encapsulated by a boundary. Jameson suggests that the experience of schizophrenia aptly describes the state of postmodern subjects in general. Working from Lacan and an autobiographical piece by a schizophrenic girl, he notes the inability of the subject to maintain its continuity across the "pro-tensions and re-tensions" of the "temporal manifold" (71). While nominally a dysfunction of time, schizophrenia equally presents a dysfunction of space: a failure to adhere to an external reality, to arbitrate the distinction between inside and outside, and to hold the surrounding world together in a meaningful totality. It becomes difficult "to see how the cultural productions of such a subject could result in anything but 'heaps of fragments'" (71), seeing as it is itself a "heap of fragments" without organic dimension or unity. The perception of such a subject would be an unmediated barrage of disordered stimuli whose immediate presence assaults the surfaces of the exposed subject. As Jameson earlier illustrates in his discussion of Edvard Munch's *The Scream*, the shift from modernism to postmodernism entailed a shift in the disposition of boundaries. Modernism foregrounded boundaries to the effect of fortifying the interiority of the alienated self; postmodernism grants them such vividly phantasmagoric power that they have displaced and even eroded the dimensionality of whatever volume they once contained. The horror of the "atrocious solitude" of the homunculus imprisoned in its own "sealed and silent membrane" (63) is replaced by the repulsive twist of vertigo in an environment of infinite mirroring.

While he uses space as an interpretive category, it is not clear that Jameson does not consider "space" the problem as much as the solution. He states, without inflection, that our daily life in the postmodern era is "dominated by categories of space rather than time" (64). Investigative frameworks like classical Marxism that focus on time position their objects (or subjects) of study as closed entities that maintain continuity as they pass through time; thus space raises some very difficult questions about the constitution of the object (or subject) itself: Where does it begin and end? Where are its boundaries? What differentiates it from other aspects of reality? Taking up space can, therefore, be a far more destabilizing method than that implied by dialectics, as a spatial perspective cannot assume the existence of objects prior to its analysis. While Jameson acknowledges the reactionary status of the *modern* subject's stiff differentiation, he does not want the dissipation of subjective boundaries to progress too far. The poststructuralist critics I will consult in Chapter Four contend otherwise: the new plasticity of limits in the postmodern era, they suggest, might be precisely the opening that political criticism needs to achieve a radical reformation of subjects. Theoretical mapping, like real Renaissance mapping, shapes subject and environment in a particular way that would exclude some of the very promise of the postmodern: its tendency toward flux and revision; its porousness of division; the fluidity of its boundaries. The inclusive transformations we imagine might require eradicating, radically, the ordering lines of our culture and of our selves.

In the manner of the early explorers, Jameson's ideal of monadic subjectivity is not sustained by his narrative; it might be proposed that his investigation, his "travel" (regardless of the optimism or pessimism associated with that term) *necessarily* tests his limits, and that all good research, any "learning," will always do so. As with Champlain and de Vaca, the hermetic individual of investigation is shadowed by a less self-assured narrative twin: this subject *"en procès,"* and how it came to be, is actually the subject *matter* of Jameson's inquiry. And an interesting subject it is.

What I have always found most intriguing (even exciting) about Jameson's account of postmodern hyperspace is the way Jameson describes space as a medium penetrating *him,* one that has overcome the very limits of his psychic and physical portals, one that encroaches upon him right up to "his eyes and body." The essay "Cognitive Mapping," an early draft of the argument in "Postmodernism," betrays similar concerns over the interpenetration of space and body and the connection of body and psyche. There Jameson worries that the "postmodern body . . . is now exposed to a perceptual barrage of immediacy from which all sheltering layers and intervening mediations have been removed" (351). This account appeals to me partly because of its obvious eroticism,[11] and partly because it describes so well the experience I undergo while traversing all kinds of public spaces—not only postmodern ones, and not only when I am lost. Jameson's comments strike a chord in me: I recognize this state; I enjoy its representation at the same time that I feel ambivalence about the state itself. The crisis of boundaries I undergo in public spaces is, on the one hand, detestable (and for me probably more than for Jameson, a sign of the physical, as well as the ontological, dangers I face). On the other hand, I experience it as a continually promising phenomenon. It is a sign of a real and vital contact with an outside and an "other," and an opportunity for a substantial interaction and personal transformation. The apparent surprise that this experience imposes on Jameson, as opposed to its familiarity to me, leads me to posit a gender differential in spatial negotiation. One feature of his spatial anxiety

[11]In "Some Notes towards Thinking about the Spaces of the Future," Gillian Rose concludes that some theorists align postmodern spaces with the feminine. She cites Harvey to point out some common traits of the postmodern characterization of space: "frothy, seductive, fecund, disruptive, charismatic, local, passionate, titillating, bound into places and blind to the global gaze" (78). I can see Jameson's distrust of the postmodern landscape as connected to a masculine unease with the fluidity and compelling slipperiness of female sexuality. And yet, what makes these men uncomfortable seems to be not so much the radical instability of the environment as the crisis of borders it seems to produce in them—the way, it could be said, this environment feminizes them. Is postmodernism enabling some kind of subterranean opening up, exchange across, the borders of the territories of sexual identity?

may be the way this space makes his body *become* conscious to him, an occurrence that is unusual, as he is accustomed—far more than the early explorers, no doubt—to forget the body, to use orienting principles that allow him to erase his physicality. For women in the West, this "forgetfulness" is much less available (and comes as a real relief when it does occur). To become conscious of embodiment could only be a positive step for masculinity, as much as such consciousness is also a perpetually wearying aspect of femininity.

A colleague of mine commented concerning this essay that a woman would never be lost as Jameson is: she, because of the ever present threat of physical attack, is always quite conscious of the position of exits, darkened stairwells, and blind corners. Her testimony does not indicate that she is any better "located," in the teleological sense Jameson intends, than he, but it does suggest that "orientation" is not a generalizable project. Space can be negotiated on a number of different levels, and for different reasons. Jameson often refers to his new program as "cognitive mapping"; apparently he assumes that cognitive maps will reintroduce a common ground of perception and understanding. But will a standardization in theorizing spaces exclude, once again, the concerns of subjects who don't fit the model of "universal" subjectivity? As subjective as the essay on postmodernism may appear to be, Jameson on the whole rejects the personal and the phenomenological. He prefers scientific mapping to older forms of orientation, like the sailor's itinerary, which remain too subjective and ungeneralizable by being tied to specific places and routes and individual intentions (90). In "Imaginary and Symbolic in Lacan," he objects to the phenomenological trend in cultural studies, the increasing interest in analyses of the "lived experience of time and space" (378), because this mode of existence reflects only Imaginary functions. We must wonder what power a politics excluding the everyday and the "personal" would have in accounting for women's oppression.

This text falls short, finally, not for its failure to include all subjects, but rather in the very exclusive–inclusive form it attributes to the subject—a form not suitable to describe the dynamics of some non-dominant subjectivities. Mary Ellen Mazey and David Lee, in their comprehensive book *Her Space, Her Place: A Geography of Women,* both define cognitive mapping and demonstrate the disparities that can exist between cognitive maps. From Yi-Fu Tuan, Mazey and Lee take the example of a married couple strolling on a shopping expedition.[12] Though both are (objectively) occupying the same space, the two may not see or hear the same things; their worlds converge only occasionally when the one asks the other to " 'admire some golf clubs in the shop window' " (37). The man and the woman may be forming the space around them in such wholly opposed ways, Mazey and Lee contend, that it would be fair to say that they are in different spaces.

Let me imagine for a moment the way this landscape might appear to the characters in their traditional couple: for the man, I imagine that the most prominent feature of the landscape would be pathways, along which he projects himself, making his world a space that returns to him a self-image of movement, command, self-assurance, and self-satisfaction. For the woman, and as a woman, I imagine a world structured not by pathways but by obstacles, the people in the landscape may be threats as much as impediments (rather than seeing how to get from "point A" to "point B" I often see what is keeping me from getting there).

My hypothetical "male" perspective may apply only to those men who *are* accustomed to dominating their landscapes: white, youngish, physically able professional-class men. Certainly teenage men could not be accused of being ignorant of the attitudes others (especially peers) project toward them, and men in poor urban areas of America cannot afford to be. But I would also argue that men of almost any class or race enjoy the luxury of being far more selective in their environmental attention than women from the same demographic group. This is true not only because they are at lesser (perceived) risk of physical attack, but also because of the customary difference of men's and women's labor—even when both are professionals.

Men's work tends to be localized, attached to particular places and time periods. That is, when men are "off work," they are not working. Women—even those who do not have children—are often responsible for the maintenance of the household's physical environment. They are rarely "off work" when at home. Men can separate themselves from their environments, live in a space that somebody else creates and maintains, "tune out," see in the space only what it pleases them

[12]From Y. F. Tuan, *Topophilia: A Study of Environmental Perception, Attitudes, and Values*, 62.

to look at.[13] Women, the working class, and people of the third world create the environment *for* Western men, so they are able to expel it from their consciousness. A woman's consciousness is more immersed in her surroundings, which she—more than a man—is likely to be monitoring for danger or for dust.[14]

There may prove to be, then, different forms of relating to space than those implied by mapping, ones that continue to be practiced today by those people who literally cannot afford to separate themselves from the ground: the indigenous, the indigent, women (until recently), and especially, I think, children.[15] Mapping excludes these subjectively variable perspectives on epistemology, but more importantly, it ignores the variability of subjective structure. Formulating the "subject" as an individual with preset boundaries, it fails to rec-

[13]One of the finest analyses of gender-differentiated modes of spatial existence comes, not surprisingly, from outside the academic community, as well as from a feminist: from columnist Jacqueline Mitchard's series "The Rest of Us." Her article "Men Still Fail to Pick Up on All the Pieces" (*Milwaukee Journal,* 30 July 1989, p. G1) provoked much of the thought in the preceding paragraphs.

[14]Mazey and Lee provide two fascinating pieces of data that may have a correlation to this divergence in subjective stance. They point out that the enormously profitable genre of romance fiction—supported mainly by women—is practically synonymous with its depiction of exotic locales (44). This suggests to me two things: first, that women want to travel, but are compelled to do it vicariously from the safety of their homes (on this supposed safety, however, Mazey and Lee relay the data of a 1978 study showing that 32% of rapes occur in the victim's home [44]). This dependence on fictions suggests that women have a much harder time escaping mentally, and therefore require outside support. In relation to the difficulty women have in escaping, Mazey and Lee refer to another study showing that "women, more than men, rate highest those vacations which would make them carefree, adventurous, daring. . . . Though both women and men rate stay-at-home vacations low, men were more enthusiastic about them than women" (45). This divergence suggests, again, that men more than women are able to divorce themselves from the environment of the home. These data come from C. Rubinstein, "Survey Report: How Americans View Vacations," *Psychology Today,* May 1980, pp. 62–76.

[15]My research comes on the heels of a furor over the failure of public education to successfully train youths in national and global geography. Children develop naturally a precise and complex knowledge of their "home" territories, however narrow that "home" may be. Given that so few children will have an opportunity to intervene (for better or worse) in world politics, is teaching them geography not simply a way of adapting them to the multinational military–industrial complex, without giving them the tools to change it? Is it simply a way of reproducing the exoticism of different spaces?

ognize the very conventionality of the individual boundary that it imposes.

The "crisis" in subjectivity that Jameson depicts may be largely a crisis only for those subjects who previously were able to establish dominance over their surroundings. The journals of the Renaissance explorers show the hermetic form of individualism to be a historically contingent fiction. Jameson's work suggests, further, that that subject's time has passed. Are we all (or should we all be), then, "becoming minor," "becoming woman," in Deleuze and Guattari's terms? "Woman" or "minor" might be the right word for this new (or old) permutation of the subject in space, especially if the Enlightenment model of subjectivity was found to be proper to a (hopefully) dead era when white, male Westerners maintained supreme cultural dominance.

It is tempting for me, from here, to posit the alternative superiority of a "feminine" or "minor" epistemology, one involved in a relationship of mutuality with its objects, not requiring the repressive "othering" of the bodies it seeks to know. Some poststructuralist critics, among them Deleuze and Guattari and Michel de Certeau, have developed theories of minoritarian epistemology; similarly, feminist critics such as Evelyn Fox Keller, who gives a fine discussion of Barbara McClintock's research in biology (in *Reflections on Gender and Science*), have adumbrated research methodologies based on an intersubjective model. (Jameson's essay itself might stand as an unexpected example of this form of research. The knowledge produced by his essay stems not from the global cognitive maps he calls for [and never actually produces], but from his personalized description of navigating the postmodern environment.) I will not follow this route, for several reasons: First, as my representation of "feminine consciousness" suggests, I am not so sure that "feminine" consciousness is necessarily a good thing, *for women*. A "feminine" subjective attitude enables (invites? testifies to?) violation as much as sharing. To adopt this consciousness as an intellectual stance may have promise, but this new epistemological formation is far from formalized, and taking it up would mean abandoning the terra firma of the established epistemological domain (in which women have yet to gain a foothold) for an as-yet mystified "feminine" practice. Second, to adopt this feminine posture also reinstates some very traditional gender divisions aligning the feminine with the "intuitive, emotional, engaged, and caring"

(Hawkesworth, "Knowers, Knowing, Known" 337); the flexible, adaptable, and soft. I will continue this evaluation of the consistency of the feminine psyche in Chapter Five.

In spite of my critique of maps, I have been far from sacrificing, throughout this study, an "objective," distanced, even superior, position. Mapping can make us conscious of big divisions, larger patterns, and how we are situated in global divisions. It allows us to measure our relation to boundaries already set up. Moreover, to return to the space of the subject, it is difficult to imagine intentional activity taking place without assuming, somehow, a coalesced subject. Jameson asks, "Does it [postmodern space] not tend to demobilize us and to surrender us to passivity and helplessness, by systematically obliterating possibilities of action under the impenetrable fog of historical inevitability?" (86). The immobilization depicted in the preceding question is uncannily similar to the disorientation described by Champlain, yet more important than their superficial similarity is a serious question. How can thought or movement take place in an environment devoid of differentiation? We may wish to denaturalize and dematerialize imposed boundaries of all kinds, but as political theorists, we certainly want to maintain goals, and not immerse ourselves in the cultural morass we already inhabit. We might inquire whether a mapping function could take place without the necessary constitution of a "mapping subject," an encapsulated ego severed from its environment. Such a possibility seems to ground Mohanty, who, in the preceding chapter, saw the map as a productive ensemble situating the dispersion of "points" of subjectivity. But again, this flat or pointillist conception of subjectivity seems to evaporate the weight and substance of subjectivities. As I noted in the preceding chapter, boundaries are often more than arbitrary: their surfaces can contain, illustrate, and shield the existence of massive, tangible differences in intentions and interests that may emerge with murderous force when those limits are attenuated. Maintaining boundaries has seemed to many theorists a necessary element of political activity.

Jameson's essay distributes the space of the subject in two opposing categories: on one side lies the securely bounded ego of the Enlightenment, a construct allowing instrumental operations but preventing substantial change and seemingly setting subjects into immutable hierarchies; on the other, a fleeting, fractured, postmodern subject no more able to formulate intentions and maintain interests than to maintain one proper unified shape. In Chapters Four and Five, I will suggest ways that these two models of subjectivity might be, if not reconciled, then at least pushed aside to discuss in more detail the ways that boundaries might be both maintained and altered to allow political redefinition of the environment. Before I get to that point, however, I would like to press further the very proposition of speaking of the subject in terms of space, and make once more the connection between the shape of the subject and the spatial environs it produces/occupies, by turning to the modern period, and the transformations in social, geopolitical, and psychological spaces that were occurring then.

CHAPTER THREE

Freudian Fabrications

DE-FORMING MODERN SPACES

It would go against all postmodern doctrine to posit an original plenitude, existing at some inaccessible point in the past, during which each "man" and each country was a bounded, internally coherent, autonomous, and unproblematic closed unit. But while the subject may in some ways "always-already" have faded, it would be foolish too to overlook a focus on and problematization of subjectivity that began with the 19th-century romantics and reached a sort of critical mass with the advent of modernism at the opening of the 20th century. The moment the subject—or any other entity—becomes the point of concentrated attention, it begins to blur, to lose the solidity it appeared to possess when it was taken for granted, or not made conscious at all. A close reading of Freud will show that the deterioration of the space of the subject posited by Jameson was already well under way at the turn of the century.

Interestingly, this period also witnessed a marked transformation in *real* space. The reformation of environmental spaces and the reconfiguration of the space of the subject are two intimately linked facets of the general cultural upheaval we call modernism. The change in concrete space could be summed up as a shift from "center" to "margin." It has to do with the relocation of emphasis outward from the heart of unified but barely conscious geographic entities to the now highly conscious distinctions between geographic territories in contest. This shift of emphasis took place simultaneously on the continental, national, cultural, and local scales.

World history is not my area of expertise, yet a little historical data may serve as an introduction. The Spanish and Portuguese colonies in South America were some of the first to detach themselves from the European hold, and the process was comparatively bloodless (largely because the cultures and governments there had already been so modified by European contact): Brazil was claimed for Portugal in 1500 and achieved its independence in 1822. Colombia achieved independence from Spain in 1819. China saw major violent uprisings against European and Japanese imperialism in 1900 (the Boxer Rebellion) and again in 1919 (the May Fourth Movement). Various European powers occupied parts of the Indian subcontinent in the 15th, 16th, and 17th centuries, but British rule was not consolidated there until the first half of the 19th century. In the second half of the 19th century and the first half of the 20th, India was the scene of increasingly violent reactions to British rule, with major rebellions occurring in the 1850s and 1919. India held its first independent elections in 1937 and finally extricated itself from a direct British rule of 90 years in 1946. The autonomy of African countries was not intensively struggled for and achieved, for the most part, until after World War II.

During the preceding centuries of exploration, colonization, and imperial exploitation, the relationship between Western and other worlds took place in a simplified spatial schema. Europe (and later the United States) sent out its envoys, its traders, its edicts, its ideology, and to it returned raw materials, goods, labor, and a little stylish exoticism. But this was not a relationship with a true "other" (regardless of how exoticized the peoples of these foreign lands may have been—or precisely because they were so); the foreign lands remained "out there" both spatially and conceptually. They did not take part in a national dialectic. The relationship between Europe and its others was not a binary, but instead a unity that projected and introjected "the other" at its own will. (Real persons, and persons with power, are beginning to make this idealized synthesis less and less possible.) Much like the mythic Cartesian ego, the European dynasties, especially those of France and England, existed solitary, as if in a vacuum, enclosed comfortably within their own geographic and ideological national identities, to which the colonies—and even other European entities—related as mere *supplement:* economically indispensable, but cognitively extraneous. (Germany, of course, always suffered anxieties of identity, but this national obsession was, until the German states

were unified under Prussian leadership in the late 19th century, probably more critical to its statesmen than to the majority of its population.) Boundaries remained relatively unproblematized and the
global hierarchy relatively persistent.

As one "colony" after another began to actively fight for its independence, the first world powers had to contend with something new,
something previously unimaginable: they were confronted by an
"other." As the colonies began to call attention to their presence, as
national and international travel became ever more commonplace,
Europe and the nation-states within it were forced to locate themselves
on the global map; confine their expansive, unnoticed egotism; and
become self-conscious. In terms of national self-conception and cultural identities, they became newly sensitized to their boundaries. The
military, economic, and cultural waves they had been sending out to
anonymous others were finally returned, turned *back,* to give them
an unwelcome introduction to their own limits. As Edward Said notes,
"Europe and the West, in short, were being asked to take the Other
seriously" ("Representing the Colonized" 223).

Certainly, America had declared independence as early as 1776, but
America—the white America that challenged the Crown (not the
native population)—was also part of the first world, albeit in adolescent
form. But America was having its own identity crisis, was beginning
to feel its own limits. America had never previously been a prime
practitioner of expansion. Within its own continental limits, it was
nothing *more* than expansion, both economically and in its own
cultural imagination (as Frederick Jackson Turner's 1893 *The Frontier
in American History* documents). By the later 19th century, the continental bounds had been reached; the 1890 census declared the frontier
closed (Kern 164); America had achieved self-containment and was
beginning, across this vast but limited expanse, to manifest a saturation.
Hence its "other" was no longer the nebulous unknown ahead, but
the articulated difference inside, between states and counties and towns
and individuals (immigration and abolition, too, played their parts).

The same process was occurring in Europe. As populations grew
and the form of capital began its (final?) evolution, increasing contact
between neighbors (both national and intranational), entities that had
once been relatively isolated, occurred. I am referring both to the
transformation from an agrarian to an industrial economy and to the
growing nationalist sensibility of European states, of territories newly

seeing themselves as "adjacent," jostling each other across boundaries that were beginning to seem all too subtle. People more frequently came in contact with "strangers" (both from within and from outside their native domains) formerly kept distant by the simple fact of geography. On both the diplomatic and the personal planes, "identity" was rapidly turning from a function of self-synonymy (organic, internal, mythic, naturalized within a territorial specificity) to a function of "difference," of comparison to newly obtrusive others.

On both levels, but especially in relation to the individual subject, one of the primary forces of this transformation was the development of technology. Stephen Kern's excellent study *The Culture of Time and Space, 1880–1918* documents (through reference to literature, philosophy, artists' manifestos, and a plethora of cultural and historical records) how the invention and popularization of such devices as the telephone, telegraph, bicycle, motorcar, airplane, iron and glass architecture, and the rail system permanently warped the traditional sense of space, blurring distinctions of near and far and inside and outside, compressing distance and bringing into contact formerly inaccessible terrains. According to Kern, "Developments in transportation generated a freer movement of people across national lines. The airplane pierced the wall of frontiers and wiped out the military significance of fixed fortifications" (194). Around the turn of the century "global travel was becoming more accessible to the ordinary tourist" (230). Technically, "travel" denotes the movement of individual bodies across and through distinct territories. However, the "massification" of travel (the spread of travel to larger and larger portions of the population) gives the effect that it is not individual bodies and consciousnesses that are moving, but space itself. The distinctions between widely separated geographical entities lose their meaning as disparate sites themselves come together in a plastic network making proximity and separation relative and mutable. Likewise the telephone and the telegraph, which, while they had little to do with the propulsion of bodies and objects through space, nonetheless leveled the significance of vast differences in time and space. Kern notes that "the telephone permitted businessmen to buy and sell from afar without leaving their offices, and at the same time expanded their 'territory' and forced them to reach out further. It brought people into close contact but obliged them also to 'live in wider distances' " (216). Likewise the rail network: in Kern's words, "railroads ended the sanctuary of remoteness. Wheat farmers were sucked into the mainstream of national and international markets by railroads that united the land masses to sea lanes in a single commercial unit" (213–214).

The importance of this "liquidation" of space cannot be overestimated. Whereas once location may have seemed a dependable, stable thing—one's body, one's place, gets its sense of groundedness by a long-standing attachment to a locale—at this time "location" becomes a matter of investigation and negotiation. As with colonial expansion and the increase of travel, communications technology caused space to simultaneously contract and expand: the areas in which people effectively lived and acted enlarged at the same time that the distinctions between discrete locations dissolved. Additionally, while "foreign" places were increasingly incorporated into the individual and cultural European consciousness, they entered there as "foreign," separate, opening up a kind of internal otherness or awareness of an outside and far away that had not been so insistent when the bulk of colonial interaction took place across the distancing expanse of the sea. The increase of intercontinental movement closed the imaginative gap between places and put adjacent spaces into an elastic flux of priority and presence.

Kern connects changes in lived space to the mutation of philosophical space underwriting the social and political order: "One common theme [of late-19th-century thought and practice] was the levelling of traditional hierarchies. The plurality of spaces, the philosophy of perspectivism, the affirmation of positive negative space, the restructuring of forms, and the contraction of social distance assaulted a variety of social orderings" (315). Kern demonstrates how real transformations in space interlocked with (he does not posit a causal connection) modifications in the aesthetic and scientific perception of the real and with political and popular conceptions of the self.[1] The emerging visibility, the "presence," of numerous distinct, coexisting, equal areas corresponds well with the nonhierarchical "democratic" philosophy of governance gaining ascendancy in Europe at

---

[1] It is hard to explain, without recourse to simple causalism, the transformation of space in such disparate fields as science, the arts, government, and technology. Concluding that it is neither a matter of quotationism nor direct influence, Derek Gregory struggles purposefully with these interconnections in chapter six of his *Geographical Imaginations*.

this time. He sees the transformation of space as homologous with the decline of the old aristocracies. Space was being denaturalized. As with the interpretation of language at a later date, the "sign" was withdrawing from the referent, and significance would be determined by the comparison of one marker to another, rather than by the linkage of a spatial concept with a dependably material ground. The nature of place, too, would be determined by its position within an abstract economy of relations.

In *The Railway Journey: Trains and Travel in the Nineteenth Century,* Wolfgang Schivelbusch gives a much more intensive and speculative analysis of technological modifications of space and their effects on the cultural and personal (un)conscious. Schivelbusch views the development of the rail system, and material innovations that resulted from it, as the prime force in the deorganicization (or denaturalization) of space. Implicit throughout his text is the assumption I have been foregrounding: prior to the industrial era, spaces—among them those of the body, the psyche, and dispersed topographic sites—were closed containers manifesting an affinity to some natural origin, outgrowths of some topographically grounded center. Technological development, epitomized in the rail system, disrupted the old stabilities. According to Schivelbusch, "As the space between points—the traditional travel space—is destroyed, those points move into each other's vicinity: one might say that they collide. They lose their old sense of local identity, which used to be determined by the spaces between them. The isolation of localities, which was created by spatial distance, was the very essence of their identity, their self-assured and complacent individuality" (45). "Spaces" are rudely wrenched from "places" and set into a circulation in which boundaries seem more crucial because they seem less dependable. Schivelbusch, like Kern, draws correspondences between various registers of spatial formation, viewing the 19th century in its entirety as an age of "the annihilation of time and space" and of the formation of a "new spatiality" (13). In the industrial era, the land heaved and shifted, detaching itself from its timeworn groundings.

More than Kern, Schivelbusch perceives a causal link between mechanization and the reorganization of human consciousness. He does not overlook social change, noting particularly the shuffling of the classes and genders in train compartments, and the ideological and material strategies developed to deal with this new permutation of social division. But besides transforming the way subjects were organized, Schivelbusch argues, rail travel transformed the way *subjectivity* was organized.

Any artificial means of motion—horseback riding, for example, or travel by horse-drawn carriages—would dictate new strategies of perception, but the phenomenological adjustment required by railway movement proved to be far more extreme. In walking, running, and riding, the perception of the landscape has a physical correlate in human muscular activity. To a lesser extent, the same is true of animal propulsion: the cart jogs, sways, creaks; there is a sense of bodily displacement that matches one's actual spatial displacement. Older transport technology preserved the traditional space–time continuum; in Schivelbusch's words, "Organically embedded in nature as it was, that technology, in its mimetic relationship to the space traversed, permitted the traveler to perceive that space as a living entity" (43). Rail travel divorced body and psyche from their customary attachment to an external geographic space. The velocity of rail travel was an experience for which travelers were initially unprepared; indeed, they received it as an assault on the physical and psychic body. As travelers gradually became accustomed to the new experience, however, they were able to develop new forms of attention, new structures of consciousness, which Schivelbusch labels "panoramic vision." They achieved an artificial mediation between "inside" and "outside," a distinction suddenly and newly critical. Following Freud, Schivelbusch holds that passengers developed a more durable "psychic shield," an improved deflector for excess stimuli. The technological developments of the 19th century brought about a transformation in the structure of the psyche. The new form of transportation inaugurated an era in which the psychic boundary—whether reinforced or ruptured—became newly conscious and highly problematized.

Both Kern and Schivelbusch comment upon the growth of cities as another factor in the transformation of space in the modern period, but the best theorist to turn to on this issue is Walter Benjamin (all three cull ideas from Georg Simmel). In his various essays associated with Paris, the arcades, and Baudelaire, Benjamin traces another shift in the layout of space: the compression, massification, and deindividualization of the space properly one's own. Prior to urbanization, there were cities, but the cultural consciousness was formed in a landscape less densely populated, in which persons, homes, and towns were spread out across an unsaturated landscape, each with a goodly amount of space between them. "Identity" was effected in relative solitude. With industrialization, great numbers of people were thrown together in the growing urban centers. More importantly, perhaps, with modernism the site of cultural consciousness shifted from country to city as the population did. An identity once founded on solitude in open space, privacy, and centrality relative to an un-populated environment had to redefine itself in relation to masses of obtrusive, impinging "others" who could be ignored only at one's own peril: one's neighbors were "right next door," separated not by a wide margin of space but only by a narrow wall or alley; a carriage, a bicycle, might come careening out of nowhere unpredictably into one's path.

The ultimate example of the new spatial relations and the new consciousness that they imposed is represented by Benjamin in "the crowd." There, individual identity was dissolved as subjects adapted to a new space and a new pace. The urban subject would be a partici-patory subject—both inside and outside its own skin, newly invested in an exterior environment that reciprocally penetrated *it*. One could resist adapting, following the model of the *flâneur*, who sauntered slowly down the street, letting the crowds part around him, as if he were still located in the less enlivened, more cohesive space of the country manor. The *flâneur's* elegantly artificial behavior acted as a force field repelling the frenetic activity around him. Benjamin main-tains that the city dweller will have to develop a "protective covering" over his psychic portals to defend himself against the overwhelming interventions of the spatial spectacle. Both Schivelbusch and Benjamin point out that, before industrialization and urbanization and the cramped hallways, rooms, and railcars that attended them, people were never " 'put in a position of having to stare at one another for minutes or even hours on end without exchanging a word' " (Benjamin, "Motifs in Baudelaire" 191; he is quoting from Simmel but the source is not specified). Both authors suggest, then, that in modern spaces, subjects temporarily floundered; losing the previously obvious distinc-tion between "inside" and "out," they erected arbitrary boundaries to rescue the psyche from its susceptibility to disorientation and worse. Limits that had once arisen naturally were challenged and redeter-mined consciously, conventionally, and artificially.

The subject, like space itself, formerly might have had a character of relative impermeability, closure, and distance from its "others" (objects, environment). Modern technologization and urbanization broke that organic compact. Identity becomes a matter of a fragile difference. "Meaning," "presence," relocates in the precarious balance across "self" and "other." While it is questionable whether the subject ever possessed the impermeable self-containment it appears from the perspective of the late 20th century to have had, the new technologies and new social relations made the lack of that dependable limitation painfully obvious, painfully conscious. The space of the subject was opened out to investigation, to interrogation, and to new critical fabulations. (David Harvey's *The Condition of Postmodernity* seeks to show how the deformation of space I tracked as a new part of modernism accelerated further, starting about 1970—leading us into the vertiginous postmodern environment explored and mapped by Jameson.)

I have attempted to argue that the modern period was one, as Marshall Berman puts it (following Marx), in which "everything solid melts into air." Space really was changing: though no doubt the layout of continents and oceans, mountains and rivers, will remain fairly consistent regardless of human intervention (though even a catastrophe of that order is no longer unimaginable), all of the permutations of space within the realm of human perception were transcending their previous groundedness, rearticulating themselves in a fluid and dynamic economy in which boundaries became a highly contested property. The move could be characterized as a passage from a logic of "identity"—encapsulation in an organically formed, internally homogeneous field, figurable in terms of a circle or sphere—to one of "difference"—the rapidly shifting, unstable movement across a single line dividing the now-equalized territories of interior and exterior, self and other, here and there. Perceiving an entity as a closed circle positions it superior to and detached from its correlates. The thing rests durable and solitary. Fashioning it instead as one side of a flat field bisected by a line, separated from its other half only by a fragile margin, sets the original entity up in a resonant and unstable tension prone to flux, reversal, and uncertainty. Leveling hierarchies puts the original "center" into a precarious plasticity liable to swift transmutation.

Partly in relation to the pressures of the outside world, partly in response to an internal development of the history of ideas, the space of the theorized subject was undergoing a comparable transformation. The desubstantialization of the subject can be traced in the work of Freud. I will depend for the most part on just two of his many texts:

Civilization and Its Discontents and *Beyond the Pleasure Principle*. These texts, and the philosophical development of which they are representative, are *symptoms* of the changes taking place in the material realm of space on all kinds of registers. They take on a life of their own, however, and dialectically influence our perception of space and the subject in the late 20th century. The uses to which Freud's theses are put by poststructuralist theorists will demonstrate that the decomposition of space can have utopian implications. Breaking down the barrier between internal and external space has been one way that contemporary philosophers have envisioned remodeling cultural space and reality itself.

Freud's "science" was founded on an attempt to provide the first rigorous description of the interior of the social individual—the common psychic substrate of cultural agents. I choose to describe his project in such awkward phrasing for a number of reasons: first, numerous critics and philosophers, from Aristotle to Locke to Nietzsche, have thought and written about what might be called the "exterior" attributes of the subject, its civil and ontological status. Moreover, the affective or intellectual processes of the person have hardly been ignored: Shakespeare or Rousseau or any other number of poets and thinkers devoted much attention to qualifying the emotions and other internal states of the subject. Their forays provided, as Freud regularly testifies, a basis for Freud's more detailed examination, and created, as Foucault might argue, the very existence of such a matter for Freud's later formalization.

But Freud opened up a whole new terrain for study by materializing the interior of the psyche, giving it a structure and a substance whereas before it had a mysterious, ephemeral, dense or vacant character. He studied the psyche as an *interior space,* seeing it not as solid or object or origin, but as an open bounded environment occupied by warring factions (conscious and unconscious), and incompatible "personae" (id, ego, superego), supported by a dynamic but also somehow stable framework. In an important way—important because his characterization of the subject is now dominant, not only in contemporary criticism but in our popular self-conception—Freud converted subjectivity *into* a space, a walled arena, a bubble both occupying all visually perceivable persons and, in some ways, forming an interior world that cuts each person off, making him or her relatively independent of the external world. Freud shifted the site of focus: it would be possible now to conceive of "personhood" totally separate from an environment as the inside takes on the dimensionality of its own independent world.

Freud's work represents, then, the culmination of the kind of subjectivity idealized in Enlightenment individualism. Explicitly and in great detail, Freud opens out, and then charts, the separate, hidden territory of the mind. But this space, no less than the other denaturalized spaces of modernity, does not remain stable, does not retain the uncomplicated empty-circle form evident in the Enlightenment ideal of the individual. Freud's psychic space balloons, mutates, fragments, stretches, fades. He simultaneously and continuously complicates the space he creates. Freud's work exhibits a crisis of subjectivity and the perception of subjectivity that aligns with the crisis of space marking the later 19th and earlier 20th centuries. It also stands midway between the untheorized monadic capsule of the Enlightenment individual and the fleeing, fluid, or fractured space of postmodern conceptions of the subject which I will address in Chapter Four. In rereading Freud, I will be concerned to show how his work is poised across these double and incompatible directions: on the one hand, to solidify the space of the subject—solidify it in *terms* of space—and on the other hand, to disrupt, dissolve, radicalize the space with which it begins.

Freud figured "the subject" quite variously, of course, and it would be senseless both to deny the contradictory nature of his figurations or to suppose that those contradictions do not persist.[2] The contradictions in his depiction of the subject have very much to do with

---

[2]This disjointed approach to the subject has been if anything reinforced by Lacan. He insists—even more tenaciously than Freud—on the insistent presence of the unconscious. Yet in his early essays "The Mirror Phase" and "Aggressivity," particularly, the unconscious is not positioned as the basis of subjectivity. Rather, he focuses on the differential spatial structure formative of "I" which, no matter how highly problematized or spatially disjunctive, would seem to encapsulate the unconscious and surpass it as the more inclusive site of subjectivity. Lacan's later work is much more consistent in its occupation of unconscious processes, which are depicted as the fundamental and obtrusive—if also denied—locus of subjectivity. The "I" that once was something like the container becomes a displaced phantasmatic object projected by the unconscious. Lacan's interpreters likewise remain undecided in tracing out his location of "subjectivity," with some working into an ever deeper accompaniment of the flow of the unconscious, with others balancing across the disjunctive inside–out of the function "I," and still others externalizing the subject as the place of the culturally spoken utterance and making the unconscious the dustbin of cultural/ideological repression, a realm initially outside the subject and rather foreign to the drives. Where do we locate the Lacanian subject?

location, the site on which he is focusing, which may be variously subject-as-ego, subject-as-consciousness, subject-as-unconsciousness, or a combination thereof, for instance, when he is analyzing that slippery entity "the mind" in *Beyond the Pleasure Principle.* Moreover, it is important to acknowledge that Freud himself does not use the term "the subject" which, in current parlance, has the advantage—or disadvantage—of seeming to include both the psychoanalytic "subjectivity"—with an emphasis on internal processes, the fantasy world of the unconscious, the interface of body and psyche known as libido—and the more political or sociological term "the subject," with its exteriorized gaze, concerned with cultural positioning, social interaction, and discursive processes. In some ways, these two emphases cannot be collapsed. On the other hand, Freud's work also ranges across this territory, at times directed toward the wholly antisocial, nearly inaccessible logic of the drives, at other times expanding outward into cultural critique (e.g., in *Civilization and Its Discontents*) and the system of social prohibition and demand.

His own construct of "the subject," then, could be said to occupy a discontinuous space, one broken up into not easily assimilable parcels whose distinctions he fails to address. Freud develops at least three topographies for the psyche, each of which can be, or is, depicted in spatial terms: there is the tripartite dynamic structure of id, ego, and superego; the archaeological layering of unconscious, preconscious, and conscious (with perception sometimes added); and the more streamlined enclosure of inside and outside that seems to contain the subject as a whole. He made various attempts to combine these three topographies, but as the sketch in *The Ego and the Id* (1923) demonstrates, they do not fit easily together (24). They are three independent and in some ways contradictory methods of perceiving subjectivity.[3] I choose to retain the term "subject" in discussing his work because it seems to be the most inclusive term available, allowing a flowing linkage between categories—the mind, the psyche, con-

---

[3] I feel compelled to provide an explanation of my "fast and loose" conflation of the various words associated with "the subject": subject, subjectivity, the psyche, identity, the self, consciousness, the mind. My near-synonymous use of these terms must be repellent to some Freudians, many Marxist scholars, and all Lacanian critics. But Freud himself, and his translators, often use these terms interchangeably. In *The Ego and the Id,* James Strachey points out that "the ego" is a shifty term, sometimes referring to the self as a whole, sometimes to a more specialized and circumscribed object/function within the psyche (8). The territory of the psyche had not yet been radically divided

sciousness, the unconscious, the individual—that might otherwise end up philosophically estranged. Our theory cannot consider itself responsible until it can account for all of these aspects of being in some (not totalizing, but) articulating framework.

Freud begins *Civilization and Its Discontents* (1930) with an apparent adherence to the model of hermetic autonomy evident in the Enlightenment individual. In response to Romain Rolland's sensitivity to states of fusion and ego dissipation, he avers that "I cannot discover this 'oceanic' feeling in myself" (12) and states that "normally, there is nothing of which we are more certain than the feeling of our self, of our own ego" (13). He implies that, under nonpathological conditions, we each will be consistently confident about our subjective borders, the place and limits of the self. In *Civilization and Its Discontents,* Freud figures the mind in similar terms more evidently related to space. He pictures it as the at-first fenced and then walled city of Rome (17). In *Beyond the Pleasure Principle* (1920), as in *Civilization and Its Discontents,* Freud figures subjectivity in terms of an enclosed, nonproblematic space: "Let us picture a living organism in its most simplified possible form as an undifferentiated vesicle of a substance

---

by Freud into "interior" and "exterior." He calls the ego a "frontier creature" (*Ego and Id* 56), making it comparable to consciousness (though he also deems it largely unconscious.) He describes the ego as a surface entity, but also as the projection of a surface—equating it with the skin of the body, as he did in *Pleasure Principle* (*Ego and Id* 26). It would be interesting to ask what kind of criticism we would possess if the two territories now reified as "interior" ("the unconscious") and "exterior" ("the subject") had not been so radically dissevered (and represented now in two different fields, psychoanalysis and cultural criticism). Freud seeks to account for them in combination. Moreover, it would be interesting to ask how the American reception of psychoanalysis might have been altered if in place of that obtuse term "the ego," "das Ich" had been translated as "the I."

These comments are necessary to explain why I give so little space to the major object of his philosophy, "The unconscious." While it is certainly the most innovative and radical concept introduced by Freud, the unconscious is also a category largely peripheral in many of Freud's writings, particularly the ones that have most interested me, which seek to characterize the more apparent dimensions of subjectivity: the coming-into-being of the individual, the "I." He frequently seeks to accomplish a description of subjectivity as a whole; when he does, the category of the unconscious remains fairly submerged. The unconscious, to be sure, undermines the conscious parameters of identity; nonetheless, each unconscious is still the property of a recognizably singular subject (regardless of the extent to which the features of the unconscious are relatively constant across subjects of a similar familial or cultural heritage). Perhaps it is just my "Americanness" speaking, as I do want a cohesive, if multilayered, and more tangible definition of the subject with which to work.

that is susceptible to stimulation" (20). In each case, Freud appears to be speaking not only of the ego, but of the subject as a whole. The unconscious is absent here, or at least well submerged; in relation to the self, the sense of "I," the mind, the human being as a whole, Freud's favored image is the inside–outside dialectic, the bounded space.

In the image of the spheroid we can see, again in its most simplified form, the spatial schema of the Enlightenment individual. Uncomplicated by distinctions within, this organism drifts in a likewise undifferentiated (either empty or full to saturation) environment. Initially, Freud's picture of subjectivity equates identity with unity: self-synonymy, organic primacy, in relation to which "otherness" is irrelevant or extraneous. In each example—the three from Freud and the schematized one of the Individual I have suggested—the self appears as a delimited area, a space defined by a border, the relatively streamlined circle or sphere. Other subjects are likewise enclosed within circles, and between subjects there are pockets of empty space, vacuums or voids. Freud's most simplified image of the subject participates, then, in the stable, organic space of centralized identity proper to the premodern cultural milieu.

But, as Yeats intoned, "the center cannot hold." I have been setting aside the unspoken context in which most readers would have located *Civilization and Its Discontents*—its unconscious, as it were. Most readers familiar with Freud's works would know that the autonomous feeling of self Freud promotes is an illusion; in the background of both the text and the ego, the unconscious lies submerged. It emerges two sentences later. Freud continues:

> This ego appears to us as something autonomous and unitary, marked off distinctly from everything else. That such an appearance is deceptive, and that on the contrary the ego is continued inward without any sharp delimitation, into an unconscious mental entity which we designate as the id and for which it serves as a kind of facade—this was a discovery first made by psycho-analytic research. (13)

At this point the unacknowledged background is brought to the fore. The presence of the id alongside the ego sets up a resonance between two powerful entities that disturbs the clean unity of the initial figuration. Both are still contained within the crystalline boundary encompassing the self, leaving the subject—even if now split into dark and light hemispheres—an autonomous entity. The unconscious lies deep within the dark heart of a well-defined sphere. And yet, by emphasizing the undismissable presence of this third entity, Freud has already complicated the smooth binary pairs of "inside" and "out," "self" and "other," that had underwritten the Cartesian ego. Lacanian critics have more than adequately discussed the consequences in this shift of emphasis in the space of the psyche.

What interests me far more than the internal relation of the conscious to the unconscious is the relation of the individual consciousness to its outside, which, for the moment, retains its clear and unproblematic character. With the next sentence—"But towards the outside, at any rate, the ego seems to maintain clear and sharp lines of demarcation" (13)—Freud begins muddling the until-now unsullied space of the subject. He continues: "This ego appears to us as something autonomous and unitary, marked off distinctly from everything else" (13). Freud undermines the initial solidity of this subject even as he asserts it, with words like "appears" and "seems" juxtaposed with the more affirmative words "certain" and "clear and sharp." The counterpoint within his assertion sets up a dramatic tension that comes quickly to fruition within the same paragraph:

> There is only one state—admittedly an unusual state, but not one that can be stigmatized as pathological—in which it does not do this. At the height of being in love the boundary between ego and object threatens to melt away. Against all the evidence of his senses, a man who is in love declares that "I" and "you" are one, and is prepared to behave as if it were a fact. (13)[4]

[4] By prying away at this passage, however, we can see that Freud views ego autonomy *as* an ideal, and one that, as Jessica Benjamin claims, carries particular gender biases. It is strange that Freud assigns the ego melting of love to the man, when he had previously attributed "anaclitic" romantic capacities to the male sex, indicating that even in love men are able to perceive women as separate objects. It is women who, in the romantic exchange, engage in "narcissism"—loving the man not for his difference, but for the way he reinforces her sense of self. Women are thought by Freud to be generally less capable of individuation; they are inept at sublimation, have weak superegos, and seek to reproduce the primary fusion with the mother in their own relationships with their infants. It is interesting that Freud characterizes "love" as a deviant state—"unusual, though not stigmatized as pathological"—as if it were an immature phase, something that healthy men get beyond, a state to be quarantined from the rest of adult life. It seems clear to me that Freud's "model subject" is, like the Enlightenment individual, implicitly masculine: while a man might have moments of insecurity in his selfhood, it is only he who is able otherwise, when he is not being so foolish, to achieve it.

This passage—"passage" being interpretable here both as "excerpt" and as "progression"—is interesting for a number of reasons. Most relevant in terms of the space of the subject, subsequent sentences display a successive retreat from the structural fortitude Freud initially (if half-heartedly, to be sure) granted the subject. With each sentence, he chips away at the subject's retaining wall and the idea of universal autonomy (which was only a feeling in the first place). First, men in love lose it; next, psychotics and neurotics. The assertion that there is only "one instance" of the nonpathological sense of fusion is embedded within a discussion of religious feeling—hardly a deranged mental state, for many people. His "trusted friend" had already attested to his own susceptibility to this state. By the close of this section (on the next page), "we" all seem in danger of melting away. He concludes this line of argument with the summation that "thus even the feeling of our own ego is subject to disturbances and the boundaries of the ego are not constant" (14). "Our" and "the" seem to refer to egos in general, of everyone, not just persons in love and psychotics. One is prepared to believe psychic solitude to be not the norm, but itself the deviation.

Because Freud tends to view the ego as "originally all-inclusive" (*Civilization* 15–16), unaware of an outside, originating in engulfing unity, he could be accused of promoting a solipsistic, monadic model of the subject.[5] The state of infant subjectivity is comparable to the state of premodern European spaces: both are "narcissistic." Primary narcissism is a state of undifferentiation, a lack of meaning in the plane of space. According to Freud, "Our present ego feeling is . . . only a shrunken residue of a much more inclusive—indeed, an all-embracing—feeling which corresponded to a more intimate bond between the ego and the world about it" (*Civilization* 16). The psyche learns only gradually of an exterior in relation to which it shrinks. Becoming a subject has to do with becoming located, with occupying a delimited space bounded by an outside. It has to do with being caught up in a relational structure, in the distinction of two positions, from which meaning, "presence" (or at least the *feeling* of presence), arises. This "presence" is far from being established once and for all at some particular psychogenetic moment. In Freudian psychoanalysis, the

---

[5]Jessica Benjamin enters this accusation in *The Bonds of Love*.

individual subject comes into being as, and only as, a function of the instantiation of space; yet that space will always be open to compression and expansion. The bulk of psychoanalytic criticism, with its "ins" and "outs" of introjection, projection, incorporation, and narcissism, demonstrates that the borders of the psyche cannot be settled once and for all, or the place of the "real" determined with the finality of a closing door. Even though the subject now is corralled within a well-delineated space, its limits and its identity are far from settled.

In fact, while the space of the monad appears secure, even dead, by nature of its closure, it is already, by being formalized, one that is undergoing crisis; it is only when the subject is unlocated, "all-embracing," that it has the unproblematized nature attributed the Enlightenment individual. Space itself would seem to be the problem that afflicts it. Partly, this is because space once it becomes conscious is instantly problematized. Partly, however, it is also because it is not only the space that defines the subject, but the subject that defines space. The subject is an effect of space, but the space that effects it is subjective. Subjectivity is a continual process of negotiation with space, of attempting to locate and reassure one's self of one's limits and to confirm the place of reality.

Civilization and Its Discontents continues on to posit the subject as an effect of a negotiable, elastic space formed in an uncertain relation to an exterior. There is not an originary monad that needs to gain access to the outside world, or recognize the difference of it; rather, there is originally nothing, neither inside nor out. The two come into being in a single action. Selfhood is enabled by the perception of difference. In Freud's words, "An infant at the breast does not as yet distinguish his ego from the external world as the source of the sensations flowing in upon him. He gradually learns to do so, in response to various promptings" (14). One such prompting is that portrayed, replayed, rememorized in the child's game of "*fort-da*" (a hiding game, roughly "gone–here") (in *Pleasure Principle*): the mother has the ability to go *away*. The body is that which does not "go away." There is an outside, it dawns upon him; as little as he may be in control of his own organs, at least he can always *feel* them. The preconscious infant might be characterized as nondimensional, as unarticulated, as nonexistent by nature of its nondifferentiation within itself or from others. It does not exist in space; it is so wholly disseminated throughout an abstracted environment, so integrally tied up with it, that it cannot collect itself. To become a subject, to become a person, is to "learn one's place." The infant becomes a subject by extricating itself from its object world, by learning the difference between "self" and "other," "inside" and "outside," "here" and "there." But throughout life, these differences must continually be explored, examined, and reconfirmed. Subjectivity is *necessarily* and *fundamentally* a spatial achievement.

Each of these texts, *Civilization and Its Discontents* and *Beyond the Pleasure Principle,* will be dedicated to transforming our conception of the psyche. The simplistic, stylized container with which they begin will be convoluted, involuted, fragmented, layered, fissured, and dissolved. *Beyond the Pleasure Principle* attempts to represent the psyche and its mechanisms, formerly "regarded as in some sort of way *qualitative,*" in a different light, "namely, as being *topographical*" (46). In *Beyond the Pleasure Principle* Freud seeks to assign consciousness "a position in space" (18). Since he is using a graphic and pictorial schema to simulate it, the spatial form of the psyche in this text proves more accessible.

In *Beyond the Pleasure Principle* Freud discusses the seat of consciousness. Referring to the sciences of embryology and zoology, he attempts to explain why consciousness may or must be located on the surface of the subject:

> What consciousness yields consists essentially of perceptions of excitations coming from the external world and of feelings of pleasure and unpleasure which can only arise from within the mental apparatus; it is therefore possible to assign the system *Pcpt.–Cs.* a position in space. It must lie on the borderline between inside and outside; it must be turned towards the external world and envelop the other psychical systems. (18)

In *Beyond the Pleasure Principle,* as in *Civilization and Its Discontents,* the unconscious is shifted into the background. In each text, the subjective boundary defines the subject as a whole. The system *Pcpt.–Cs.* (Perception–Consciousness) provides the center of attention in this text; it becomes a kind of "character" with its own narrative of development. Freud displaces the seat of subjectivity from a mystified and solid interior to the plastic and unstable surface. The transformation this shift wreaks on the conception of subjectivity should not be underestimated. The subject's previous density will now be porous and dislocated. The subject loses the quality of distinct interiority with which it began. Its certain separation from other subjects, objects, and its environment loses self-evidence.

As the privileged site of subjectivity moves from the interior to the boundary, the boundary becomes open to question. There is a line lying on the border between inside and outside: is it, then, part of the inside or part of the outside? If it is part of the inside, what separates it from the outside? Does it require its own boundary, lying above and adjacent to it? If it is part of the outside, what then separates and contains the inside? If it is porous, what keeps the subject from seeping continually into its environment, losing its materiality? If it is substantial, how can the subject maintain access to its environment? Under close observation, the dark slash of the unilinear boundary originally visible in the image of the vesicle rapidly begins to widen into a fuzzy gray band or to multiply geometrically. This shell or boundary is only one thing, a single line if considered graphically, but one that has two surfaces: one facing inward, the other outward. This interfacial characteristic will lead inexorably to doublings, triplings, multiplications.

Like the mystic writing pad that Freud will consider in a later essay, the membrane of the subject or system *Pcpt.–Cs.* must be composed of at least two layers: "Thus we should be able to say that the excitatory process becomes conscious in the system *Cs.* but leaves no permanent trace behind there; but that the excitation is transmitted to the systems lying next within and that it is in *them* that its traces are left" (19). Already we can see a doubling in the protective membrane: the surface layer must be accompanied by an adjacent and deeper layer to receive permanent traces. This would be the place of memories, perhaps transient ones; we might surmise that below this is another layer, even deeper, and another deeper still, one perhaps not even accessible to consciousness any more—what we might call "the repressed." The subject, originally a mass enclosed by a skin, begins to look more and more like the famous onion.

Above the outer receptive layer is a third layer, one that repels stimuli. The outer layer, however, is of a different nature than the remainder of the organism: "It would be easy to suppose, then, that as a result of ceaseless impact of external stimuli on the surface of the vesicle, its substance *to a certain depth* may have become permanently modified" (20, italics added). An organism, entirely self-enclosed and nondifferentiated internally, will develop differentiation along its limit abutting on externality. The border then becomes truly a separate though adjacent article, equally the property of the external world as of the internal. Yet it is hardened only to a "certain depth," making the distinction between the vesicle and its skin not entirely clear, just as it may be difficult to identify the place where the skin ends and the body below begins. At the first layer, which sloughs off with no harm to the organism? When it begins to bleed or hurt?

> The little fragment of living substance is suspended in the middle of an external world charged with the most powerful energies; and it would be killed by the stimulation emanating from these if it were not provided with a protective shield against stimuli. It acquires the shield in this way: its outermost surface ceases to have the structure proper to living matter, becomes to some degree inorganic and thenceforward functions as a special envelope or membrane resistant to stimuli. In consequence, the energies of the external world are able to pass into the next underlying *layers* [italics added], which have remained living, with only a fragment of their original intensity; and these layers can devote themselves, behind the protective shield, to the reception of the amounts of stimulus which have been allowed through it. . . . *Protection against* stimuli is an almost more important function for the living organism than *reception of* stimuli. (21)

It is no longer a skin or a surface that encloses the vesicle, but now a "crust"—a dead matter lying atop the living matter; while it is not really a part of the organism, it is not truly removable either. The *border,* initially functioning to enclose the subject, now appears to be, in some ways, independent from the subject, to be an object in its own right. And what was initially *one* layer has now multiplied into layers of an *indefinite* number.

Not only does the boundary multiply from one layer to many, it loses its clean curvilinear structure, becoming jagged and protuberant. According to Freud, "In highly developed organisms the receptive cortical layer of the former vesicle has long been withdrawn into the depths of the interior of the body, though portions of it have been left behind on the surface immediately beneath the general shield against stimuli" (21–22). The boundary loses its distinctive location, becomes fragmented: parts of it remain lodged at the surface while others sink deep within. Other fragments "may perhaps be compared with feelers which are all the time making tentative advances towards the external world and then drawing back from it" (22). The surface traverses the body, from inside to outside, occasionally even extending into the outside world. The "boundary" ceases to act as a container. The space of the subject is dispersed across the territories we imagine to be "inside" and "outside" the subject. Its components are farflung. If the concept of the boundaried vesicle was once being used to underwrite Freud's confidence in the solitary and unary subject, that same model rapidly proves to problematize that subject.

This is especially true in that the boundary, the line that once served to keep inside and outside apart, may now serve as a switchpoint for the inside, the substance that it originally served to contain, to exchange places with the outside, the material it initially served to exclude. In addition to receiving impulses from the outside and transmitting them to the inside, this surface also receives excitations from the *interior* of the organism: "This sensitive cortex, however, which is later to become the system *Cs.,* also receives excitations from *within*" (22, italics in original). So the surface of the organism is not only turned outward; the same recording surface receives markings from within. The passage of excitation is no longer unidirectional. Excitations from either direction find this surface, not the organism's interior, as their mark. The organism can be seen as being *inside out,* with the interior of the object now acting as the environment. From the standpoint of the boundary membrane, then, how can there be a difference any longer between inside and out?

There is one difference between the boundary's relation to the interior and the exterior: from the inside, Freud posits, there is no protective barrier, no partly dead "scab" to protect the consciousness from excess excitation, as there is on the outside. Thus,

> a particular way is adopted of dealing with any internal excitations which produce too great an increase of unpleasure: there is a tendency to treat them as though they were acting, not from the inside, but from the outside, so that it may be possible to bring the shield against stimuli into operation as a means of defence against them. (23)

The boundary, already ambiguous as to its situation on inside or outside, thereby becomes a more complex matter: excitations arising from within can seem to be *more* outside than those arising from without. The subject, once cocooned safely inside its dead shell, can extrude into the environment, like the boundary itself doubling, multiplying in identity and location. The idea of the subject as the space of interiority has become inconceivable.

One line with two surfaces becomes an organ with two functions: both to join the organism to reality (in acting as a medium of transmission) and to repel an excessive amount of reality (as a membrane of protection). The problem here is that the boundary, the *Pcpt.–Cs.* layer responsible for perceiving and judging the difference between inside and outside, is also responsible for maintaining the difference between inside and outside. Thus it is not so much a line *around* the subject, containing it, as it is the line *between* self and world, that which by differentiating them, creates them. "Reality" was in the beginning identified with an objective position in space, that which lay outside the boundary. But it is the organism that dictates the location of the boundary and allocates the contents of the different spaces (not consciously, to be sure). "Space" may have been the medium in which the vesicle (and the subject) originated, but as the organism develops, it is the organism that determines the layout of space. "Reality" is established through a management of space, but that space is projected by the subject. Throughout this and others of Freud's texts, and as a result, throughout the body of psychoanalysis as a whole, this problem of identifying the place and nature of reality will continue to appear.

Freud locates the genesis of the reality principle in the pleasure principle: "We know that the pleasure principle is proper to a *primary* method of working on the part of the mental apparatus, but . . . it is from the very outset inefficient and even highly dangerous. Under the influence of the ego's instincts of self-preservation, the pleasure principle is replaced by the *reality principle*" (4, italics in original). Freud here suggests that the subject is originally controlled, motivated, and organized only by the pleasure principle, which has no relation to reality, that is, to the external world. Originally, the distinction between interior and external real world is created by a psychic process; the external world is nothing more than a phantasmic space, a construction of all the subject's unpleasurable experiences. As an offshoot or outgrowth of the pleasure principle, how could the reality principle—which is still a principle, a part of the psychic mechanism, and not an organ reaching into the outer world—be anything but distorted? The reality principle will be a continual process of determining what *is* outside the self, a continual process of manufacturing a distinction between the two spaces, and of buttressing an interior so that there can *be* an "objective" reality. "Reality," then, initially the obvious "outside" of the subject, loses its place; it becomes that which is constructed through a continual production of the distinction between inside and out.

I began by positing that the dematerialization of space taking place in Freud's texts mirrored that taking place in the real social landscape of modernity. In each, organic and centered spaces were being denaturalized and accelerated into increasingly elastic configurations. It is now possible to reverse the comparison: the real spaces of modernity exhibited the same characteristics as the "space" of the Freudian subject. Untethered to their organic groundings, they became an effect of human mediation. They took on a character of being subjectively *produced,* denaturalized, immaterially constructed, arbitrary. This is true of national and geographic entities, as well as of personal environments. As I argued in Chapter One, "national" identity is now less a function of geographic origin than of semiotic arbitration (as much as political entities may try to fortify their claims by reference to original occupation). It is increasingly clear that "nation" issues less from an adherence to a natural terrain than from discursive—and real—warfare.

It would be possible, if we pushed Freud's arguments in *Civilization and Its Discontents* and *Beyond the Pleasure Principle* to their logical conclusion, to evacuate entirely a "real" of space and make all of space a projection. While I believe that material spaces are radically susceptible to the touch of ideation and signification, the tension between "real" and "subjective" is one that I want to maintain and explore for a moment, if only to reconstruct their relation otherwise. I have pressured Freud's texts beyond their own intentions; Freud himself does preserve the status of an objective reality, no matter how open to interpretation that reality may become. In spite of the contortions to which he subjects the space of the psyche, Freud holds on to an ideal of a solid and normative dimension for the subject. At the opening of *Civilization and Its Discontents,* Freud refers to pathological states "in which the boundary lines between the ego and the external world become uncertain or in which they are actually drawn incorrectly" (14). By saying that there are cases in which the boundary lines of the ego may be drawn *in*correctly, Freud implies that there are other cases—nonpathological ones—in which they are drawn *correctly.* He leads us to see the psyche as a container of predetermined dimensions, which any given person may fail to fill or may overflow; nonetheless, the "correct" size and shape of the ego preexists us and acts as a standard. It would seem that the space of the subject in *reality* does not necessarily match up with the ideal space laid out for it in philosophy, theory, and common sense.

The opening of *Civilization and Its Discontents,* then, features a bidirectional pull, on the one hand to marshal the psyche into a defined space and on the other to explode or liquidate the space of a psyche already far too settled. Freud, like Descartes, seems to maintain the ideal of autonomy more as a reassuring illusion than as a descriptive fact. It is almost as if he posits it to stem the anxiety brought on by his own uncertainty about it. While seeming to want to hold ego autonomy as the standard, the remainder of the text breaks down the circle of the self; while seeming to want to assert ego-fluidity as a norm, Freud retains a commitment to the monadic priority of Individualism.

Freud's work on the subject is posed in terms of space that consistently mutates from a stable organic space to a destabilized, abstract space that cannot be contained within the bounds laid out for the Enlightenment individual. Freud's picture of the subject relies upon space and problematizes it, in the same way that space was becoming a problematic, complicated category in reality during the industrial and modern periods. The reason for this transformation in the space of the subject is Freud's increasing focus on it, his increasing problematization of it. While Freud clearly intended to transform our understanding of the individual, I do not believe that his juggling of the space of the subject was intentional. Rather, he used the language of space in order to achieve a more accurate picture of subjectivity. He sees language as an immaterial medium for describing a real structure.

"Real," however, is a shifty term, and no less so in Freud's texts; it is never clear whether the "space of the psyche" that he depicts is an ideal or a material category. Freud's depiction of the psychic structure in *Beyond the Pleasure Principle* is tied to that other shifty term "the mind," which can refer both to a physical organ, the brain, and to that more intangible thing, subjectivity. Clearly, at some times he wanted to locate the space of the subject in a material structure. Taking the "vesicle" as the basic model for subjectivity, Freud draws a parallel between the nonmaterial psyche and the structure of the material brain: "Indeed embryology . . . actually shows us that the central nervous system originated from the ectoderm; the grey matter of the cortex remains a derivative of the primitive superficial layer of the organism and may have inherited some of its central properties" (20). Freud suggests that the outermost layer of consciousness, synonymous with the outermost layer of the brain, derives from the skin. Indeed, the difference between the two objects, psyche and brain, immediately becomes indistinguishable: "It will be seen that there is nothing daringly new in these assumptions; we have merely adopted the views on localization held by cerebral anatomy, which locates the 'seat' of consciousness in the cerebral cortex—the outermost, enveloping layer of the central organ" (18). This conflation of the psyche and the soma is understandable, as it is difficult to imagine the psyche except as something "housed" in a body, and even more difficult to do so after the invention of this metaphor, which so easily takes on the appearance of reality in Freud's text. The subject as it is normally discussed in psychoanalysis is or should be far removed from the concerns of brain biology. Subjectivity, while attached to bodies, also can be separated from them—in language—and deviate from them, psychically. Equating the psyche with a physical structure, collapsing the space of the psyche with the space of the brain, or making the subject coterminous with the body, will reintroduce the graphics of the subject that underlie that subject-as-individual: unary, coherent, and bounded.

At other times, however, Freud seems to want to disassociate his theory of the subject from a material foundation. In *Civilization and Its Discontents,* he mocks himself for drawing physical parallels for the psyche. Casting about for an image that will represent the way repressed materials can remain alive in the unconscious, he turns to the image of the Eternal City (which I discussed earlier) and to human physiognomy. But he quickly discards these models: "The embryo cannot be discovered in the adult"; "in the marrow-bones of the grown man I can, it is true, trace the outlines of the child's bone, but it itself has disappeared" (19). He abandons his comparison of the psyche to the walled city of Rome for the following reason: "If we want to represent historical sequence in spatial terms we can only do it by juxtaposition in space: the same space cannot have two different contents" (19). Thus in the city, or in the adult's body, an earlier stage of development may appear as a trace, but it cannot coexist, be equally present, as can the earlier stages of psychological development that are preserved, unmodified and intact, if buried, in the mind. It would appear that Freud is renouncing his temptation to employ the language of space—of sites, bodies, volumes, areas—because it is too material; it fails to capture the reality. He chides himself: "Our attempt [to compare the psyche to a city] seems to be an idle game. It has only one justification. It shows how far we are from mastering the characteristics of mental life by representing them in pictorial terms" (19).

But is it really space that he renounces here? Or is it only the conventional, bounded, solid space underlying organic entities? When he says that historical sequence can only be represented by juxtaposition in space, that "the same space cannot have two different contents," one way to read this statement would be to say that space, graphics—that which can be figured in a picture—and the psyche are incompatible; to use space as a figurative medium is only a convenience, a way of grasping something otherwise intangible. However, in rereading this sentence, what we see is a privileging of space over time. What is wrong is not that the spatial picture cannot represent the historical process, but that the historical process erases important aspects of the spatial reality. It is not the *substantiality* we associate with material spaces here that fails, but the very *insubstantiality* that is effected by the passage of time. In the psyche—unlike in the history of the city—the two contents *do* coexist, whereas in history one supplants the other. In the psyche, two contents *can* occupy the same space; it is the factor of time that disappears, that has no meaning. Freud wants to preserve the dimensionality of space but surpass its conventional physics, so that two objects *may* occupy the same space.

It is toward developing such a medium that much of Freud's writing endeavors, as will Einstein's in a different field. The poststructuralist critics I will be studying in the next section strive even more markedly to disrupt and refigure the space of the subject; the question is why.

As a way of answering this question, it will serve to return once more to the issue of whether the psyche really is a space, and if so, how. It is clear that though Freud was ambivalent about comparing the psychic structure to material ones, he intended his account to carry descriptive veracity. He saw the subject—whether figured as psyche, consciousness, or organism—as a space.

Of course the psyche is a space, we want to say; don't we always talk about how we feel "deep inside," don't we feel invaded by those who impinge on our privacy, don't we have our "expansive" moods, and don't we feel that expansiveness crushed when others are thoughtless or overbearing? Don't we "retire into ourselves" when the pressures of social interaction are just too much to bear? Many psychoanalysts and psychoanalytic critics, in the object relations school as well as in more Lacanian or philosophical disciplines (the names of Julia Kristeva and Jessica Benjamin come to mind), analyze the subject even more apparently as a function of space. One author, Didier Anzieu, has written a marvelous book, *Le moi-peau,* enlarging upon the Freudian theme of the subjective space; his argument is that subjectivity is an effect of the psychic "skin," the boundary between inside and outside; the subjective frontier is the place of consciousness, of affect, of reaction, of all those things that go to make up the moment-to-moment sense of "I." Disruptions in the psychic membrane—locating it incorrectly, in ways that do not correspond to the socially consensual "place" of the subject—indicate psychosis.

Surely, we live our consciousness as if in three dimensions, at the very least distinguishing between "inside" and "outside," our appearance and how we really feel. Possibly, the more neurotic, or at least the more "self-conscious," one becomes, the more convincing is this feel of space: we may feel ourselves to be "locked inside our heads," isolated from others, incredibly sensitized to their advances, intrusions, withdrawals. Yet if the psyche is a space, it is not a real one. Though normally identified with a body, it does not reside within any particular place in the body: that is to say, even though it is most akin to the brain, the structure of the psyche in no way corresponds to the morphology of the brain. "Subjectivity" is not reducible to the individual body; in pathological cases, the two can become quite separate (at least in the psychotic imagination). If we do live the psyche as a space, it is one that is ideal.

This is what I would want to say in conclusion about the space of the subject as depicted in Freud: indeed, the space of the subject is insubstantial, but it is a space nonetheless. In the same way that ideology, for Coward and Ellis, is material because it influences our everyday actions, the "space" of the psyche may be the only "reality" we have. Our whole history of critical and everyday language on the subject materializes the subject as a space we live.

However, if the space of the subject is a reified effect of language, it can, through other inscriptions, be changed. No matter how much the boundary of Freud becomes a convoluted, jagged, multiplied, abstract, intangible, immaterial limit, we nonetheless get the sense that it protects something intimate and weighty. The boundary may be a surface phenomenon, a sheer curtain, but behind it, to one side, press the pulsating substances of reality; to the other side, the vital density of the unconscious and consciousness. For some poststructuralist thinkers, language itself is the fine screen separating these two dimensions. Dematerializing the walls separating subjects from other subjects, objects, and reality, they guide us into a vertiginous universe echoing with possibilities for political change.

CHAPTER FOUR

Vertigo

POSTMODERN SPACES AND THE
POLITICS OF THE SUBJECT

(Hesitate)

First there is a mismatch—perception out of true with perceived: the swimming head confronted with an inassimilable depth, a failure to place the limits or judge the dimensions of an enclosing space, a failure to situate a surface in relation to the body and its surface, or the consciousness, and its surface. . . .

"Vertigo" is defined first in dictionaries—standard, *Oxford*, medical—as dizziness, but I want a more precise definition, precisely because one word apparently does not exhaust all the meanings: there is "dizziness, whirling, giddiness," but vertigo is left over—in it, there is something more.

Vertigo strikes me most frequently when I make a misstep or merely fear that I have done so. I think I have come down the last stair, and then the instant before my foot touches level ground I am sure there is *one more step* and my foot is about to meet its fate in nothingness—in anticipation of the bodily tilting I expect to feel, I undergo a mental tilting: the world and myself fall out of harmony, a gap opens up into which I could fall infinitely. . . .

It is not a pleasant sensation, this vertigo, and if it would not be too bold (a kind of faux pas) to put myself forward so carelessly I might mention that several years ago I was hit be a car (a simple matter of being in the wrong place at the wrong time—a disastrous mismatch between my intention, propelling my body, and the external

world of objects, traveling under their own forces). For months following the accident I was plagued with what the medical profession
calls "posttraumatic vertigo," a rift between the subjective dimension
and the real of space that would come over me unpredictably, or very
predictably any time I tilted my head to the left. A neurologist told
me that such experiences have no definable somatic source—there is
no verifiable injury, to the brain or to the semicircular canals that
ensure balance—and yet such phenomena are not uncommon to
survivors of gross physical trauma.

The Vietnam War popularized a new diagnostic category, "posttraumatic stress syndrome." For veterans, this condition developed as
a result of a prolonged immersion in unlivable conditions—unmanageable because unpredictable: long nights of darkness, unidentifiable
noises, sudden, terrifying blasts of activity. But the condition has causes
surpassing the immediate location, and the immediacy of it, that have
precisely to do with mediation; disorientation was compounded by
the absence of cultural recognition faced by the veterans upon returning: most had little psychological support, little acknowledgment,
little *change* in the fabric of social or imaginary life to admit the trauma
they had endured. Psychological disturbance resulted, as did flashbacks
(once again a denial of the present location in favor of a more crucial
environment of survival)—a return of the repressed, analyzable
through the mechanism of repetition described by Freud in relation
to war neurosis (and other phenomena). Since then, others—survivors
of childhood abuse, survivors of ghetto childhoods—have recognized
the relevance of the diagnostic category to their own experiences. . . .

Other people, I know, regularly experience a mild form of vertigo
when looking down from great heights, or leaning out over railings
into an undefinable emptiness, where there is no support for the body,
or at least that is the judgment the autonomous nervous system makes;
vertigo, then, can be the result of trauma, or the anticipation of the
withdrawal of support, the detachment of the subject from its physical
site, or a dissonance between subjective experience and cultural assumptions, or the unexpected mobilization of subject or location:

a feeling as if external objects whirled around the person affected, or
as if he himself had been whirled around . . . any movement or sense
of movement, either in the individual himself or in external objects,
that involves a real or seeming defect in the equilibrium of the body

and is associated with more or less disturbance of consciousness. (Funk
and Wagnalls, *Standard Dictionary of the English Language*, 1895)

Aren't things beginning to whirl a bit, becoming a little deranged, in
this dictionary's definition? Is vertigo a real defect in equilibrium or
only a seeming one? Is it the subject who spins here, or is it reality
that tilts madly? Does it denote real movement or just a false sense
of movement on the part of a deceived subject? Is the disturbance of
consciousness more or less?

Adults, to be sure, don't like this feeling, falling into it only as a
result of trauma (or uncertainty). Children, on the other hand, often
court this feeling, inducing it in themselves by spinning, arms out-
stretched, palms up to the heavens, in open spaces; or they roll down
hills, exchanging ventral and dorsal surfaces at an accelerating rate, so
that they can stand, stagger, giggle drunkenly, and short-circuit the
dependable physiological tendency to conform consciousness to outer
reality. They disjoin the surface of external physical space from the
surface of consciousness that mimetically conforms to it—because
they have only recently achieved the adherence of the two? Because
to do so feels like freedom? Because they are testing the limits of
reality, or of their own relation to reality, or because they have not
yet come to take for granted the conformity of the two, or because
the compact has not yet been rudely broken? What kind of child
would resist this dizzying experimentation?

I have introduced (and reintroduced) the idea of "trauma." Wouldn't
it be nice if etymologically the root of "trauma" were the German
noun for "dream" (*traum*)? Then it would be easy to set up a neat
equation between disorientation in space, psychological wounding,
and imaginary compensation. Representation, attempts to construct
new pictures, would come onto the scene. Couldn't we see in vertigo,
as Freud saw in dreams, an attempt to resolve, in imagination, an
uncooperative environment? See in vertigo a sign of an unmanageable
occurrence in the dimensional realm of the social, and a compensating
attempt to manage it psychically? But the root of "trauma" is just
plain *trauma*, Latin for "wounding." Representation will come into
play shortly; we need not abandon the structure so quickly. What if,
indeed, all of this dizziness comes from being stuck in a situation that
is at odds, sometimes violently, with the subject? Could vertigo—even
simple disorientation—be called the product of a certain antithesis

between the subject, and her internal spaces, and the external, material and social, spaces that she occupies?

Vertigo makes me think of other spatial disorders, like agoraphobia. The fear of open spaces: we know this to be predominantly a woman's disease. But it isn't just space itself that the agoraphobic resists. Though in French agoraphobia appears as *peur des espaces* or *horreur du vide,* "agoraphobia" in English is "derived from the Greek root 'agora,' meaning the place of assembly, the marketplace" (Doctor 12). Hence we see that the problem with space isn't just *space;* it is the fact that there are other people in it—other people who are creating it, determining it, composing it. (To wit Sartre's bitter aphorism: "Hell is other people.") Is it surprising, then, that space itself could seem a bit hostile? Agoraphobics fear leaving their homes—that space defined as the woman's place, and one that, of all the places available to her, may be most subject to the control of the individual woman (in traditional gender arrangements). In 1870, Moritz Benedikt suggested that the primary affective component of agoraphobia was not anxiety but dizziness. He hypothesized that a large part of this dizziness might stem from the fear of attracting unwanted attention (Doctor 14). Little wonder that this is primarily a woman's disorder. ("Agoraphobia" is separated from "agrophobia"—the fear of sexual assault—by only a few letters, most significantly a misplaced "o.")

We might expect claustrophobia—the fear of small spaces—to be predominantly a men's disease, since it seems like the inverse of the fear of open spaces, but in fact claustrophobia often precedes agoraphobia (Doctor 105). Perhaps a simple inversion occurs, with both conditions issuing from a generalized disturbance of spatial arbitration. Maybe, for women, space doesn't stay safely outside, where it forms a comforting environment for us to distractedly occupy. Leaving us wanting to stay inside our homes, spaces no less constituted by patriarchy, as much as they may at times seem like a haven from it? Do women, as Luce Irigaray might wonder, really have any choice in this situation? Are either of these places *ours?* Is the choice always between agoraphobia and claustrophobia, between suffocating in social spaces and suffocating at home?

In *The Bonds of Love,* Jessica Benjamin argues that to return to the logic of space, to situatedness, is to get back to the specificity of the feminine subject. Between "woman" and "space" lies some fluid margin; between the terms, and even between the two things, there occurs a slippage, a folding, or an overlap. While Benjamin (and other object relations analysts) conceive space as a particularly relevant, even adaptable, category for women, other critics see in the fluidity between women and space a sign of feminine violability. Because a woman's structure is far from settled, because she is receptive, woman remains open to invasion. Catharine Mackinnon observes of the material realm that "women know the world is out there. We know because it hits us in the face" (112). Space invades women: we can't push it from our consciousnesses. Moreover, space might seem a particularly alienating category for women, in that the conflation of woman and space has been one of the mechanisms allowing the masculine subjection of both territories. Elizabeth Grosz, following Irigaray, claims that "in the West, time is conceived as masculine (proper to a subject, a being with an interior) and space is associated with femininity (femininity being a form of externality to men)" (9). "Man" becomes self by extricating himself from both woman and space, metaphysically and metapsychologically. Space seems less easily objectifiable for women, a terrain we cross and inhabit with trepidation, a medium slipping into us against our will, one with which we blend in the patriarchal symbolic system. Between the alienation we confront in material and metaphysical space and our intimacy with it, a wavering, a distortion, or an inversion occurs. Could this be the source of everyday, or theoretical, vertigo?

Perhaps vertigo proves a particularly relevant category in relation to subjects who find themselves, by nature of the kind of subjects they are, located (and not at home) in a hostile environment. Women occupy a discursive and social space not of their own making, whose logic is structured to reflect and sustain a subject position directly opposed to their own. But I would have difficulty naming vertigo solely a feminine phenomenon. Whatever it is about dysfunctions of space that attracts feminist theorists has also attracted a significant number of male theorists, or theorists of the masculine. I'm thinking, first, of Kristeva, and her recent study of abjection: "Instead of sounding himself as to his 'being,' he [the abjected subject] does so concerning his place; 'Where am I?' instead of 'Who am I?' The space that engrosses the deject, the excluded, is never one, nor homogeneous, nor totalizable, but essentially divisible, foldable, and catastrophic" (8). Though Kristeva does not name her subject "Man," the pronouns are telling—as is her lack of concern with gender difference. Abjection has a negative quality, but states with exactly the same qualities when associated with femininity—motherhood, *jouissance,* the semiotic—are characterized positively. In fact, if other feminist philosophers view vertigo as an essentially feminine experience, Kristeva designates it a predominantly masculine state.

One could search for all kinds of reasons why masculine subjects, susceptible to vertigo in spite of their gender, seek to mobilize and achieve mobility in their cultural locations: perhaps sexual orientation, perhaps race, perhaps class are relevant. The *Oxford English Dictionary* (*OED*) tells us that "mobility" refers to the capacity to move from one location to the next, the "ability to change easily or quickly; liability to fluctuation; changeableness, instability; fickleness" (perhaps these men possess a disproportionate share of what have been designated feminine qualities?), but it also refers to "the mob," the lower classes: "*mobility*" as opposed to "*nobility*." Regardless of the reasons, social or psychic (and didn't Freud indicate that *all* subjects become repressed and oppressed in assuming subjectivity?), these subjects share a common interest in politics, and redefining space has come to seem an integral component of the political drive. "Vertigo," then, represents the experience of subjects out of step with the social order and the reality it sets up; this will be especially true if, besides occupying a subject position that our cultural logic labels "marginal," they have imbibed a heady dose of poststructural and political theory, a brew guaranteed to make them unfit to indifferently cooperate in culture's logic.

Leaning over the brink of the self, we peer with growing distress onto an alien and bewildering cultural complex. In a hostile environment, the self feels out of place, which leads to a dissociation of self from that place, and a sense of the wrongness of the self itself, in the first place (after all, as Freud indicated, isn't "the real" always that which is outside? Then it *must be right,* and it *must be* the self that is wrong). "Dissociation," I am compelled to note, refers not only to a detachment of subject from the world, but also to the deterioration of the internal ordering of subjectivity: that is, "severance; division; disunion"; "[being] cut off from association or society"; but also, "the process or result of breaking up associations of ideas"; and the "disintegration of personality or consciousness" (*OED*). The internal–external relation breaks down, resulting in a degeneration of interior organization, and finally—one could imagine, in advanced stages—in a confusion of the external order too. Things begin to circulate, and no longer know their places. Foundations and frameworks crumble and things loop and circle and shift and spin: the inside flies to pieces and explodes outward, the outside melts and fragments, and elements from both sides drift freely across an indifferent boundary. If the outside is unstable to such a degree that the subject becomes disengaged, who wouldn't want to induce the same confusion, in reality, so that inside and outside come once again into harmony?

"Vertigo"—if I am to arrest its movement in a return to a stable, denotable reality—seems to refer to three things: a rift between subject and reality, the mobilization of the internal processes of the subject, and a new fluidity of the external realm. I am using vertigo as an emblem for an increasingly common move or complex of moves in contemporary theory that center around a manipulation of space. There are multiple applications for the poststructuralist medium of space, and I want to range across their heterogeneity, for space functions in different ways for different theorists. But certain similarities arise in a common emphasis upon what I will call "in-difference," a relaxation of the boundaries parceling up "subject" and "real," maintaining separate sites within the real, and ordering the internal composition of the subject. "In-difference," in spite of its variations in application, functions always to the same end: critics manipulate internal spaces, external spaces, and the relation between the subject and external space to loosen or reconstruct the political landscape that we all, as subjects, occupy.[1]

Fredric Jameson's essay on postmodernism represents one example of the use of vertigo. Unlike Jameson, however, the majority of contemporary critics working with space seek to occupy vertigo, not to repel it; they choose even to increase it, to explore it, to extend it. Jameson, like so many of his postmodern colleagues, confronts in space the signs of an unacceptable social order. The critics I will be focusing on here invoke vertigo as a sign of the unliveability of the current

---

[1]Edward Soja and Barbara Hooper, in "The Spaces That Difference Makes," describe the postmodern fascination with space similarly, and well: "We suggest that this spatialized discourse on simultaneously real and imagined geographies is an important part of a provocative and distinctly postmodern reconceptualization of spatiality that connects the social production of space to the cultural politics of difference in new and imaginative ways" (184).

social order, but rather than banishing it, they incorporate it into their arguments, use it as a starting point for formulating new practices of intervention and a new social order. They project their perceptions of space to change the space they perceive. A counterexample to Jameson's appears in Elizabeth Grosz's use of "legendary psych-aesthenia," a condition described by Roger Caillois (and reintro-duced by Lacan). The subject afflicted with legendary psychaesthenia, a form of psychosis, exhibits a radical dysfunction in the order of space. He cannot affix himself to reality by establishing a predictable or reliable place in it. Noises and visions that seem objectively to fall outside the bounds of his body and psyche seem rather to occur within it; indeed, even his own consciousness may be detached from his body, drifting from its moorings on the inside to float outward into external space. He may see himself from the perspective of a doorway halfway across the room and really believe that's where he *is*.

What seems to attract Grosz's interest in legendary psychaesthenia (and what certainly elicits my own interest) is the idea that there might be a method to this madness. Clearly, Grosz is latching on to the bond that links space and reality, and using the disruption of space as an entry into disrupting the current cultural order. If space, that external and objective medium seeming to underwrite all of our action, perception, and thought can be redefined from the position of the subject, then reality might likewise be open to rearticulation—and not only by those people whom our culture labels "psychotic."

In legendary psychaesthenia, space from the perspective of the subject does not align with space as determined objectively. The subject has chosen his own subjective space, one that does not align with cultural expectations, but even though this is a space *defined as subjective,* he does not have the freedom to choose freely where he might be in it. Isn't this idea of the subject's "proper" placement a matter of convention and, in some ways, discipline? The culture wishes to restore him to "health" and "rationality" by resituating him in the location *it* has plotted for him. What could be gained by forfeiting the matrix of order that culture has placed upon reality in parceling it up into dependable spaces, and attaching certain affects, meanings, and organic personalities to these places?

The critics I will feature in this chapter begin with the idea that the differences that already appear in reality are imposed by ingrained habits of thought, tradition, and ideology. Indeed, there is an increasingly common move to equate power with space, and particularly to equate state power with the solidification and ordering of space. Michel Foucault, in *Discipline and Punish,* offers perhaps the most sophisticated anatomy of the State's imposition, cultivation, and management of spaces: institutions delimit different places for different activities (e.g., work and leisure); distribute different populations in different sites (the students are in schools, the infirm are in hospitals); and separate each site from the others (the hospital and the prison are allocated different grounds). Discipline draws clear distinctions between possible behaviors and subjects, replacing flux, heterogeneity, and variety with rigid difference and identity. Deleuze and Guattari, like Foucault, criticize the solidification of spaces accomplished by "State knowledge," a method of knowledge defined by its desire to cement the landscape: "History is always written from the sedentary point of view and in the name of a unitary State apparatus, at least a possible one" (*A Thousand Plateaus* 23). The state founds itself on and can be equated with "striated space," a space studded with nooks and hooks that capture flows and snag escaping movements; it is crushed within boundaries that compress mobile heterogeneities into arrested masses.

Michel de Certeau, in *The Practice of Everyday Life,* goes even further: he argues that the very delimitation of "inside" from "outside," self from environment, produces the effects of power. To impose a binary structure on heterogeneous actuality and consolidate proper spaces, one's own and that of the other, based on a clear division of inside and outside, is to gain power. Indeed, doing so testifies to a power that one already has: "Thus military or scientific strategies have always been inaugurated through the constitution of their 'own' areas. . . . In other words, *a certain power is the precondition of this knowledge* and not merely its effect or its attribute. It makes this knowledge possible and at the same time determines its characteristics" (36, italics in original). An institution, in naming itself and claiming a territory, enables itself to argue for its own necessity, its prerogative to define vast areas of the social landscape, and to define them in its own terms. Meanwhile, the individual is disempowered by the institutional delimitation of inside and outside: by conforming to culture's demand that we have an inside and an outside and make the effort to know their difference, we get caught up in the rationalization that makes the social order work, lose our capacities for imagination and freedom, and are reduced to orderly, docile subjects.

De Certeau, casting about for a political method that would escape the rigid differentiations imposed by complexes of power, finds the opposite to the state-authored "strategy" in the "tactic," a political initiative operating within a different spatial logic. According to de Certeau, a tactic is "a calculus which cannot count on a 'proper' (a spatial or institutional localization), nor thus on a borderline distinguishing the other as a visible totality.... A tactic insinuates itself into the other's place, fragmentarily, without taking it over in its entirety, without being able to keep it at a distance" (xix). The tactician "borrows" the environment for momentary pleasures or practical needs, wresting her constitution from the efficient partitioning that makes her a producer of profit and a reproducer of power structures. He finds its model in "everyday" activities (e.g., walking) that feature a fluid, transient, and active creation of spaces. The tactic's decomposition of inside and outside, its "in-difference," provides the basis for its political potential.

De Certeau does not stand alone in encouraging a realignment of the subject and its external social or material space. What *is* the place of the subject in relation to external space? There seem to be two options, both of which are inscribed in the form of relating to the world known as paranoia, which Jacques Lacan deems the true format of human knowledge as a whole ("The Mirror Stage" 3). Paranoia, etymologically, is caught up in spatial indeterminacy: its Greek roots mean "beside" and "mind." "Noia" (from *nous,* "mind") is the simple part; "para," the part having to do with spatial relation, is a little more interesting. The *OED* indicates that as a preposition, *para* had the sense " 'by the side of, beside,' whence 'alongside of, by past, beyond.' "

This figuration represents the relation we customarily suppose the subject to occupy in relation to its social or material environment. The subject appears like a pocket abutting on external space. This is the place assigned us by culture: partner, adjunct, corollary. Culture wills us to maintain a differentiation, to attain and maintain some apartness, to not go blending with exteriority in radical ways, to respect the bounds of "propriety"—the disjunctions between subjects and the circumscription of ourselves as subjects. At the same time, however, culture wants us to mirror it, blend with it, not allow our differentiation from it to become alienation or opposition: though a boundary separates inside and outside, the content should exactly replicate the milieu, setting up a homology between the two areas, a total osmosis that amounts to undifferentiation.

But "paranoia," if it is indeed representative of knowledge, puts things slightly aslant: in composition *para* "had the same senses, with such cognate adverbial ones as 'to one side, aside, amiss, faulty, irregular, disordered, improper, wrong,' also expressing subsidiary relation, alteration, perversion, simulation, etc." (*OED*). To be *next to* is not the same as being *one with:* a miscalculation, a deviation, can occur, such that we remain adjacent to social space, but "out of line." If we adapt to the assumptions of traditional thought (if we become what some of the critics in this chapter might call "state thinkers"), we might picture epistemology as a process of coming closer and closer to this external realm, bringing ourselves and our perceptions into ever closer alignment with it. However, poststructuralism has revealed the degree to which the external realm, seemingly the "natural world," is itself a product of social shaping. Trinh Minh-ha puts it well in pointing out that "thinking true means thinking in conformity with a certain scientific (read 'scientistic') discourse produced by certain institutions" (124). Indeed, the "civilized mind" has classified as "untrue" "many of the realities it *does not understand*" (124, italics in original). In the phrase "thinking true" I cannot help but hear another definition of "true": "proper alignment or adjustment" (*Webster's New Riverside Dictionary*, 1984 ed.). If "reality" is the product of ways of thinking imposed by the state, then to simply draw into closer alignment with it is to acquiesce to the social order. Hence many theorists seek instead to *promote* a rift between subject and space, to complicate their relations, to fracture the structure of epistemology—that is, to encourage individuals to become more and more para-noid.

Jane Gallop provides one example. Playing with the ambiguity of the genitive involved in the phrase "women's studies," she points out how the lack of clear position for the word "women" in this phrase

> (subjective or objective) may resonate not only with the mother as bound up with the infant prior to the latter's ability to distinguish subject and object but also with women's traditional place in culture as neither object nor subject but disturbingly both. Woman's ambiguous cultural place may be precisely the standpoint from which it is possible to muddle the subject/object distinction, that distinction necessary for a certain epistemological relation to the world. (*Reading Lacan* 15–16)

On the one hand, in this passage Gallop builds on the model of feminine intersubjectivity developed by such thinkers as Nancy Chodorow and Carol Gilligan. In the paradigm of undifferentiation apparent in this passage from Gallop, the "subject" and the "object" of knowledge can readily switch places. The "subject," as we know, has too often been designated masculine, leaving women, mothers, and earth to occupy the position of object. If the subject–object dichotomy is decomposed, however, then objects can take on the status of subjects too, thereby influencing and shaping the structure and content of the subject. They become active participants in a dialectic of knowledge based on mutuality, tenderness, and solicitousness: Tell me your desires, and I will respond to them.

However, Gallop is doing something more radical than simply encouraging a flexible and sympathetic attitude on the part of the subject: she is muddling the subject–object structure quite a bit more than might be possible by merely encouraging a status of openness, which would still maintain the subject and object as products of separate spaces, regardless of how it encourages a bidirectionality to the flow of information. If "woman" appears on both sides of the rift usually deemed necessary to define knowledge, then we as women thinkers are caught up in a structure of knowledge less akin to that found in Plato's allegorical cave (where the figures caught on the walls are mere shadows of the knower, and the penultimate moment of knowledge comes in recognizing this) than to the experience common to many who grew up in America of trailing through a funhouse, unexpectedly catching our images repeatedly caught in mirrors. When we are in the funhouse, we confront ourselves displaced, inverted, and sometimes distorted by tricks in the production of the glass. In Plato's allegory, we get out of the cave to achieve greater objectivity and clarity. But we go into the funhouse willingly to experience a state of confusion. We go into the funhouse on purpose, with the intention of deranging our usual ways of knowing. We don't attempt to achieve anything but the experience itself, so that we can occupy a place where our customary modes of negotiation don't make sense. This is a place to begin, not to produce more knowledge, but to worry the foundations of knowledge.

The assumptions underlying Gallop's statement presume that traditional knowledge has produced enough, much of it unbeneficial to the subjects it has constructed, and that it is time to start taking apart the structure that enables traditional knowledge. Gallop, like several of the other critics I have discussed, relies on the Freudian thesis that "reality" issues from the infantile moment of dividing self and other, inside and outside. Maybe by returning to this moment of primary narcissism and primary disorder, reality can be erased and then reconceptualized. Go back to ground zero, square one, the drawing board; erase it all, start again, restructure that which has been violently conformed into expectable patterns. . . . Vertigo, then, the whirling of objects about the subject and the whirling of the subject within this vortex, can be a way of clearing the ground to enable new and more flexible arrangements to rise.

Each of the preceding critics toys with the relation between subject and world, attempting to open out the space of the subject in order to change the *place* of the subject socially. They take up experimentation with space as a method for intervening in social relations; they blur the space of the subject—the margin between subject and world, between subject and subject—as a positive prospect for reconstructing the cultural order.

With the exception of Gallop, however, the preceding critics also hold to a certain objectivity concerning space: they maintain a certain distance from the vertigo they describe. While depicting and advocating a disintegration of the barrier between inside and outside, they preserve that distinction in their own writing. They preserve, in fact, a separation between language and reality. Other critics have broken down even that difference. They consider the assumption that "discourse" and "space" are separate categories to be the final frontier holding back social change.[2]

These critics—Foucault, Baudrillard, and Deleuze and Guattari provide representative examples—radicalize the possibilities of space, blurring the boundaries retaining subjects and objects or redesigning their borders in such a way that "difference" is preserved, but within a different physics; they indulge at times in (the idea of pre-Oedipal)

---

[2]It is interesting that Derek Gregory's thinking in *Geographical Imaginations* follows a parallel path through nearly identical theoretical territory: from Donna Haraway to Trin Minh-ha to Michel de Certeau, following the semiotic connections running from "cyborg" to "inappropriate/d" identities to the politics of "the tactic" in a refusal to "know one's place." Gregory even touches on the political implications of "paranoia" and "schizophrenia" as forms of knowledge. I regret that his book emerged too recently for me to engage with it—and benefit from it—in any form more substantial than this footnote.

undifferentiation but do not wholly negate difference. Nor do they perpetuate the idea of organic differentiation. The ambiguity of their manipulation of space can be captured in the hesitating caesura of the term "in-difference." In-different space is not stable enough to support vertical or three-dimensional structures, such as empires or buildings, or the Enlightenment individual. It is organized by momentary impositions of difference so fleeting that the space appears to be continually reorganizing along the horizontal plane. In-different space assumes neither subject nor objects, but creates each as a fold or bubble within its substance. The distinctions already in force disappear, lose their substance, so that the symbolic fabric of the conceptual terrain— the divides discriminating subjects from one another, the visual gaps separating material objects, the rifts between subjects and objects, inside and outside—might be reconstructed differently. Language forms the medium for making and remaking (remarking?) these differences. These poststructuralist critics consolidate "space" with discourse to form a "text-ure," a revised discursive fabric that provides a medium for immediate social metamorphosis. The phrase "in-difference" also signals the way that their praxis is inextricably tied up with transporting us into different spaces.

We like to suppose that the organization of the external world, best symbolized by the layout of the land, is natural and necessary, and that our representation of the external world merely reflects a "natural" order. But what if, instead, human patterns and mediation come first? What if they are the real architectonic forces shaping the world? Then the form of reality becomes mutable and open to intervention. Applying the destabilization of space that is possible in language to the external material world forms a bridge for mobilizing that reality.

From Jean Baudrillard, we receive a view of maps that circles back to inform Fredric Jameson's. Baudrillard opens *Simulations* with a scenario designed to induce vertigo: the Borges tale of a map of the Empire "so detailed that it ends up exactly covering the territory" but which, as the Empire declines, becomes "frayed and finally ruined, a few shreds still discernible in the deserts" (1). According to Baudrillard, however, in the postmodern age "it is the map that precedes the territory. . . . It is the real, and not the map, whose vestiges subsist here and there, in the deserts which are no longer those of the Empire, but our own" (2). Baudrillard proceeds to dismiss his extension of the Borges allegory because it still subsists upon the myth of differentiation, upon stable distances forming comfortingly discernible separate objects like "original" and "copy," or the Aristotelian fiction that the image is a reflection or perversion of a basic reality, when the cultural milieu today is more one in which the image "masks the *absence* of a basic reality" (11). Reality "is its own pure simulacrum" (11). In such a circumstance, we are stuck in a reality that cannot be superseded or abandoned for another one, one in which image and reality coexist as effects or products of a suspended, ungrounded, insubstantial system.

Gazing down on the simulated system Baudrillard lays out is like being caught in that moment of hesitation before putting one's foot down on the next step: the two surfaces (land and map, real and representation) hover in an unstable, immeasurable difference. The gap between them waxes and wanes, with their distinction wavering until one gets dizzy trying to judge their relation. The spaces and spans forming modern manageable space no longer work in the environment of postmodern circulation, where it is impossible to find any stable referent, a ground from which to measure distance and volume—any measure of depth at all. The external world takes on a dispersed, shifting, transient quality: it becomes a field of flux. Baudrillard deranges the appearance of the firmament by subjecting it to the flow of discourse and positing a new accessibility between the two realms. As with mapping, then, this is not just a metaphorical relation (the land can be compared to language) but a metonymic one: space forms an adjunct of language and acts as a precipitate of it. The postmodern landscape, settled in the first place by perceptual convention, has now opened to the reorganizational capacities of discourse. If space is only an effect of discourse, then a new way of speaking and imagining can change it. It is as if by foregrounding metaphors of space the gap between metaphor and reality narrows, the bridge is shortened, the interchange takes place that much more quickly: space itself is the aperture through which discourse can effect reality.

Baudrillard's adumbration of the postmodern environment can act as a guide to the spatial imagery, the linkage between language and space, for poststructuralism in general. For Foucault, likewise, space opens a series of doors through which discourse and the real, subjects and knowledge, can speak to each other and begin to mutually influence each other. Foucault takes the stable, deep, permanent space that constitutes three-dimensional landscapes and transforms it into a new kind of space that is malleable, transitory, and utterly flat. The first kind of space, he insists, is only an appearance afforded by a kind of philosophical Renaissance perspective. Foucault uses the language of space to highlight the formative effects of discourse and the instability of the plane it constitutes.

Foucault's analytics and politics are inextricably linked to creating an alternative physics for space. His alternative spatial text-ure both represents itself as a more accurate depiction of the real work of power and shifts the paradigmatic grounds for conceiving power. Power has generally been conceived as a dichotomous structure pairing intent and result, cause and effect, oppressor and oppressed. But Foucault levels the dimensionality of the social edifice, making power, knowledge, and subjects alike the temporary internal effects of a dispersed, evanescent field. The subject loses its organic solidity to appear like a bubble within a perpetually plastic substance. Subjects appear "in-different," neither causally prior to power's mechanism, nor imaginable outside its perpetually (re)formative web:

> It seems to me that power must be understood in the first instance as the multiplicity of force relations immanent in the sphere in which they operate and which constitute their own organization. . . . Power's condition of possibility . . . is the moving substrate of force relations which, by virtue of their inequality, constantly engender states of power, but the latter are always local and unstable. The omnipresence of power; not because it has the privilege of consolidating everything under its invincible unity, but because it is produced from one moment to the next, at every point, or rather in every relation from one point to another. Power is everywhere; not because it embraces everything, but because it comes from everywhere. (*History of Sexuality* 92–93)

Foucault's writing works to establish the supple fabric of in-different space as the true basis of the cultural order, but beyond his epistemological motive lies a political one. Producing this radically depthless and plastic substrate in discourse, he can project it back onto reality, encouraging the deterioration of persistent divisions and a new mobility in ordering the social field. If differences, once organic and rigid, turn instead to unstable "in-differences" that are the transient effects of a social structure, then a new mobility of the cultural order can be effected. What he seems to be advocating in "On Popular Justice" (in

Power/Knowledge) is the organization of practices within a different spatial logic. There Foucault argues for a new form of justice, one that could not be called a system—a dispersed popular movement rising up from the present needs of a people that expends itself immediately in the course of its own execution. Similarly, in the realm of sexuality, he argues that *sexual norms,* which imply slow, hermetic, and permanent stabilities, should give way to an economy of *pleasures,* fleeting and immersive stimuli that arise and disappear within specific limited settings ("History of Sexuality" 191). He implies throughout his works that were Western society able to think in terms of the diffuse and multiple instead of being compelled to collect fragmented existence into sensible, ordered groupings and wholes, our world would prove far more egalitarian.

Deleuze and Guattari, in *Anti-Oedipus* and *A Thousand Plateaus,* have offered one of the most radical reconceptualizations of space. They dissolve all stable "reals"—the subject, its objects, the placid and granite extension of spaces—and rearticulate them in a modified universe of rapidity, movement, speeds and slownesses, reversible distances, atomized particles, transient coalitions, and escaping aggregates. Their theory depends on space without relying upon its usual coordinates of depth, distance, volume, and direction. Shooting through the turgid "striated space" of the State are "lines of flight" that "deterritorialize" the static blocks of the State apparatus, softening its stable structure, if only momentarily, before the State remasses, "reterritorializes" into a different arrangement on a different plane. Deleuze and Guattari attempt to imagine operations in space without resorting to constricting form; they want to grasp movement at its most fleeting, before it has been weighed down by the arresting baggage of structure; indeed, objects would be only the summation of all kinds and speeds of movements totaled into one sum. Their "smooth space" is "in principle infinite, open, and unlimited in every direction; it has neither top nor bottom nor center" (*A Thousand Plateaus* 476). Their intent is not only to reveal this recombinatory property as the true space of the subject, but also to advocate this form of subjectivity as a healthier model that would permit the life of desire within capitalist society for longer and longer periods of time.

Deleuze and Guattari never exactly locate what it is they're talking about when they talk about things such as "lines of flight," "deterritorialization," or "smooth" and "striated" spaces. Are they speaking of discourse, concepts, or materiality? Breaking down the walls between these categories is, in part, the point of their project. "Striated space" refers to order: the fact that we think in straight lines, drive between lines, and build sidewalks in straight lines. "Lines of flight" crisscross these lines, escaping them, leading us on mental flights of fancy, such that we lie around drunk in doorways, so that upright citizens have to walk around us; or we write poetry, or we block the streets surrounding the White House, diverting traffic. All of these actions, for them, can be equated in that they all subvert, divert, escape around, or tangle the structure that culture imposes. Their writing leaps out of the stark moonscape of traditional philosophy and darts up into the cosmos, refusing to adhere to party lines and to conventional differentiations.

Deleuze and Guattari's philosophy is itself a "line of flight" that the subject who reads or writes must occupy, becoming like a ray, or must travel along, to escape the suffocating densities of traditional thought. A reader either conforms to it or departs—no critical distance is imaginable within it. To be caught up in their text-ure is destabilizing; the subject finds the conventional differentiations that supported her eroding beneath her feet. Her mind, the very substance of her thought, reshapes to their very novel pattern. When I read Deleuze and Guattari, I become a different kind of subject, conformed by intensities, flows, contacts, rather than my usual ponderous autonomy. I too am freed from the constraining baggage of cultural structures and feel more powerful, imaginative, uninhibited. This effect derives from their style as much as from their philosophy, both of which are an effect of their vertiginous "phantasmaphysics" (Foucault's word). Revolution, they claim, is an inherent effect of inhabiting the spatial plane they devise.

Deleuze and Guattari center their reinvention of space around a critique of the Oedipal model in *Anti-Oedipus,* where they introduce the term "the body without organs," whose mechanics will be further developed in *A Thousand Plateaus* (where it is often abbreviated to "BwO"). They empty the depth of Oedipus, dissipating his status as full volume and dispersing him into a multiplicity of "desiring machines." In their hands, the subject is flayed and bisected, turned inside out, taken apart, and reconstructed along the lines of temporality and desire.

The central example of the desiring machine in *Anti-Oedipus* is the breast–mouth machine, a whole in which two components are intimately and perfectly, though not permanently, matched, without a gap of "lack" or "unconscious desire" left unfulfilled. The breast–mouth makes up a unit, a temporary assemblage; it is not the parts of other wholes (mother, baby), but a working synthesis in itself and for its own purpose. The breast flows; the mouth draws the flow off. The body without organs is the place of presence, action, and registration of stimuli for the subject before its space has been differentiated into distinct organs and areas, each with their own purpose and solidity; it is the place of connection to other bodies and other features of the world, where we "deterritorialize" the territories set up by the State apparatus and are in turn cyclically propelled into new combinations and spaces. It would be unsafe to consider the body without organs a single visible object like the "real" body, for such a reading of the body depends upon the traditional spaces of closed containers and full volumes. "Subjectivity," the central substance of the subject in traditional philosophy and psychoanalysis, appears as something like a by-product along the margins of the body without organs. We are currently only partially BwOs; Deleuze and Guattari's project is to help us become fully, continuously so.

I focus on Deleuze and Guattari because their deployment of in-different space is ultimately not only perceptual and polemic but also pragmatic. They intend it as a praxis to be followed or as a structure to be occupied. For their own part, Deleuze and Guattari are not trying to get us (as readers or as a culture) any*where* except deeper into smooth space, for that to them is "revolution" in itself. The seriousness with which they offer up their version of "in-different" space makes their work an ideal site for beginning to pressure the poststructural redefinition of the space of the subject as a whole.

For Deleuze and Guattari, the body without organs is incapable of being dis-satisfied, since it is not endowed with intentions—desires tending toward absent objects—but rather is based on interconnection: the accomplishment of a "machinic assemblage" with other sites and part-objects. The body without organs cannot be a site of lack, nor one of presence. Such categories become meaningless, as does the entire notion of a complete "subject" with political or personal

interests of its own, *beyond* a recombinatory property. Deleuze and
Guattari's analytic possibilities could not reside in a space already
occupied by the objects precipitated in the state's binary machine, like
"man" and "woman," or "inside" and "outside." The ideal state of
the body without organs would be a kind of accelerated, orgiastic
fragmentation and multiplication quite in excess of the boundaries
between subjects and objects already established by conventional wisdom. This figuration of, or plan for, the body may give pause to some
critics, especially some feminists (myself included) from many differing
perspectives.

While their program of deterritorialization and desire may appeal
to me on a *personal* level (I would like to live my life like that, or at
least like to pretend that is how my life is lived), what form does it
offer my political aspirations? Their reconceptualization enables a view
toward the microphysics of desire and a departure from the idea of
the subject as *essentially* lacking, but it causes me to hesitate: sometimes
I really don't get what I want. In their view, this could only mean
that what I really wanted was to be left unsatisfied. Does their view
take into account the reality that the outside world may not cooperate,
that other people bring to our meeting desires that might diametrically
oppose mine? Does it give me a way of changing their desires, or
only a way of recognizing my own? Does it help me achieve those
desires? Does it make some of the desires I have—to walk the streets
unmolested, to get a job, to change laws (almost anything requiring
intention)—illegitimate?

I can imagine boldly striking out on a daily basis, ever attentive to
my desire and the way that it succeeds in incremental forms (I eat a
banana, becoming like a mouth–banana machine; I run or jog, becoming like a body–pavement machine): but what happens when,
wrapped up in my infantile omnipotence as I deterritorialize the
landscape, and it deterritorializes the surface of my body (and this
does happen—I become less "woman running through park" than a
skin–air combinatoire, a sunshine–flowers–consciousness coalition,
dispersing outside the boundaries of my identity and the sac of my
skin—for sure, I am not trammeled inside of it): what happens when,
as today, I encounter other people?

The air–skin assemblage that I was turns back into a woman, a
woman beginning to think she was being rather egotistical and careless
assuming she could just run through a city park because that was

where her desire led her. My outside world doesn't cooperate, doesn't convert into smooth space just because that's what I've "become." (And what if those things I feared did come to pass? I clutch the attacker, coupling with him, recognizing that the circuit of desire is being completed, becoming subsumed in a Molly Bloom–like chorus of "yes's"; and besides it's useless to conceive the world in those outdated terms of positionalities, "man" and "woman," which hold no sense in this environment of transaction, movement, speeds and slownesses.) Don't we know, as women, that some kinds of contacts, some expressions of desire, are not willed by the party touched? Who benefits from such a practice? Alice Jardine observes (somewhere in *Gynesis*) that such a politics has seemed particularly attractive to young male graduate students, who take up the Deleuzian program with a passion. Is not this turn toward deindividualization and declassification simply a way for immature psyches to return to pre-Oedipal omnipotence, when they could be undisputed masters of bathtubs, small toys, animals, and mothers? As pleasurable a prospect as this may appear from *my* perspective, what misery I would live if others directed it toward me. *A Thousand Plateaus* is consistently plagued by the worry that a "line of flight" may turn just as smoothly toward fascism as toward liberation. That is, I think, an appropriate concern.

Current political realities test the limits of theory in ways that it cannot yet manage. Deleuze and Guattari's work represents a familiar poststructuralist drive to eject the "objective" perspective, the distanced, uninvolved, external, focal point underwriting mapping, the "third term," or authority (be it the law, the father, or the phallus) in favor of a processual, unstable, diffuse immersion in difference. However, it is not clear (equally so in feminist paradigms that would negate the law of the father in favor of the arbitrary mutuality of mother and infant) what would then guarantee an ethics. Contemporary theoretical challenges to hierarchy locate subjectivities or part-subjectivities in a flat terrain, leveling organic dimensionality and dematerializing the walls that served to separate former "identities." But recent world events suggest that on a geopolitical scale, as on the personal scale in which I have located my criticism of Deleuze and Guattari, boundaries may protect us as much as they confine us, or may protect even as they confine (the traditional cloak of femininity, which positions us as "weak" and "fragile," wards off certain kinds of insults and assaults, even though it is itself a kind of insult; the borders of former Eastern European states, while arresting cultures in what they considered disadvantageous relations, at least warded off violence). Equalizing the members of binary pairs, leveling hierarchies, and destroying the boundary may be necessary to promote equality and the transformative knowledge of the other, but violence may be its necessary price. Poststructural theorists tend to see the current stagnation of culture and offer in-difference to counter it; focusing on the present situation, we have yet to consider the fallout of our plans once implemented. However, by maintaining space as a certain grounding, I propose, critics give away their desire, which is less to evaporate positionalities in an all-out war negating arbitration than to expand the scope we currently occupy, pushing back the frontiers of dominant spaces that have been historically overbearing. Across the fragile boundaries space preserves, the subject can take a larger hand in reforming reality without having to suffer its submersive incursion.

The problems that arise in attempting to employ Deleuze and Guattari's framework can act as a standard for the possible blind spots in the poststructuralist reordering of space as a whole. Adopting in-difference can come too close to adopting a position of indifference (the two are separated only by a fragment of a line): it can lead subjects to disrespect the bounds of others, or to cede too much of the social territory and lose the capacity to maintain their own self-interests. Moreover, while representing itself as a method for intervening in the form of the social, it runs the risk of banishing the subject from the social and leaving it isolated in its own fantasy. Many of these writers seem inexplicably attracted to, even in favor of, the kind of disjuncture between the subject and the real evident in psychosis. Grosz's interest in legendary psychaesthenia or Deleuze and Guattari's in schizophrenia can stand as examples. Is the danger here that we change the space of the subject, the mental landscape, instead of affecting the external world? Do we change our ways of thinking, change ourselves, and think that amounts to changing culture's articulation of spaces? Does changing the *space* of the subject, theoretically or psychologically, magically represent an intervention in social constructions of the real? While proposing that discourse and real space are mutually formative, theory naturally enough locates discourse as its site for intervention. But does *writing* differently, formulating a new "text-ure," amount to changing the social fabric? These questions can be followed out in Foucault's notion of local politics.

For Foucault, as for de Certeau and Gallop, knowledge forms an inextricable element of the state's composition of spaces: it is the very method by which the determination of space occurs. Epistemology—the medium of contact with outside space—cannot, then, be separated from space. Reshaping epistemology becomes the very method of rearticulating social spaces. Just as Foucault collapses the divisions between subject and discourse, he eliminates the distance between the agent and the social field. The intellectual need no longer, and should no more, take the role of the adviser—that is, a position *outside* the struggle, above and beyond and ahead of it. The intellectual exists immanent to a system; absorbed in it, his activities make its surface tremble as he influences it and it saturates him in a mutually absorptive involvement. Objective distance of analysis (posed in terms of the binary) is replaced by analysis taking place from within a mobile network. The subject's action is necessarily and perpetually political; politics is not a gesture toward a separate realm. Similarly, renegotiating on the level of scholarship—theory—has an effect in the realm of theory, and that is its place of action, not "outside" in the "real world." Reforming the space of conception appears its own politics.

Foucault and other thinkers such as Deleuze and Guattari leave their philosophies open to the charge of idealism. In their promotion of "in-different" spaces, the critics I have been working with often fail to differentiate between, or may even seek actively to destroy the differentiations of, discursive and material spaces, discursive and material actions. Indeed, that has been their purpose: to open the physical and social environment to theoretical intervention. It cannot be denied that Deleuze and Guattari's reconceptualizations of praxis have had substantial effects, for example, in Guattari's treatment of psychotics in the mental institutions of Paris, nor that Foucault performed a different kind of political activity outside the academy in the prison reform movement, or that their theories have drastically influenced academic methods. However, it seems that many of these critics see new forms of writing and thinking as the very essence of political activism. They locate a transformation of reality in their own process of conceptualization. I fear that they overestimate the power of academic discourse and the reach of intellectual influence—and thereby substitute for an intended effect on the real a shadowy imaginary compensation. In the end, some differentiations of space—like those "inside" and "outside" the academy, inside and outside theoretical discourse—might prove unavoidable.

Jane Gallop, at other moments an advocate of in-difference, likewise draws back from its excesses, reclaiming the difference between the "inside" and the "outside" of the subject as necessary to action. Gallop points out that advocating "fluidity" runs the risk of being no more than wishy-washy. Gallop puts these fears this way in *The Daughter's Seduction*:

> I hold the Lacanian view that any identity will necessarily be alien and constraining. I do not believe in some "new identity" which would be adequate and authentic. But I do not seek some sort of liberation from identity. That would lead only to another form of paralysis—the oceanic passivity of undifferentiation. (xii)

What seems to make Gallop hesitate is precisely that indeterminacy I located in Deleuze and Guattari. Undifferentiation on a psychic scale can at times be pleasurable, and therefore desirable, but totally negating boundaries makes it impossible to move, or to tell when one has moved. (I would pressure Gallop's lack of pressure on Freud: though he certainly characterized undifferentiation as a totally immobilizing state, there's no guarantee that it is so. Babies move all the time, as we can easily observe; while their motion may not connote intention, it is, as Deleuze and Guattari would surely contend, movement nonetheless.) While some kind of activity may occur, it could not be measured in terms of plans or goals, which seem to require (at least metaphorically) some distance between a beginning point and a conclusion, the closure of which signifies success. In political terms, as well, entirely sacrificing boundaries—such as that between "man" and "woman"—makes impossible the usual political tasks of identifying group interests and seeing them through to realization. Conventional though they may be, it may prove necessary to preserve the bounds of the subject to make political action imaginable.

Through their "text-ure," contemporary theorists attempt to transport us. However, it must be noted that while exploring in-different space, each of these critics remains grounded in space. Space offers qualities that seem contrary to the otherwise total fluidity that these critics offer. It connotes difference and distance, location, separation, and limitation at the same time that their theories radically foreshorten such solidities, temporally and corporeally. Additionally, none of these critics sacrifices a stance of oppositionality; while emphasizing the utopian (etymologically, "not" "a place") prospects of undifferentiation, none of these critics succumbs to the inundating flood of the surrounding culture. Though softening or opening the subject's limits, they retain a certain critical difference, or critical distance, indicating that Fredric Jameson's imperative for mapping may remain impossible to resist—and foolish to dismiss. Hence it might be valuable to ask what kinds of limits still exist within in-different philosophy.

Certain distinctions remain or should be maintained between the spaces of the subject. The first among them might reside between psychic space and discursive space. From de Certeau and numerous other critics we receive the Freudian idea that the division between inside and outside on the part of the individual psyche provides the foundation of reality. Starting with this assumption, many critics propose breaking down this difference in order to reconstruct reality. However, while the dichotomy of internal and external space may found reality for the *individual* subject, it is far from being the basis of reality on a *social* scale. The boundaries that instate cultural reality—borders between objects, sites, subjects, and groups of subjects— are created largely in isolation from the boundaries necessary to formulate individual egos. These social boundaries occur in discourses and institutions, and while such institutions have a concern with making individual egos conform to their articulation of the social field, such divisions also can take place in the absence of subjective cooperation. In other words, whether or not I am willing to align my edges as subject with the frontiers of the category "woman," culture and the other subjects in it will do it for me. Opting out of the system of cultural reality does not necessarily mean that it will exempt *me*.

As the theorists I have dealt with in this chapter have argued, discourse, physical space, social location, and psychic framework flow into each other supplely. By softening the fixity of the discursive landscape, they attempt to ventriloquize change in the social realm. However, as my charge of idealism toward Foucault and Deleuze and Guattari suggested, I remain unconvinced that the interchange of (academic) discourse and (political) reality can take place quite so easily, simply by wishing, or writing, it into existence. If the real is nothing more than the accretion of discourses, it has become real due to long practice and popular "consent." As academics, we refuse to sacrifice the possibility that changing discourse can change the way we live, but we must delineate their means of interchange more complexly. How discourse might achieve such a reformation of the shape of the subject will be examined in the next chapter, where I return to a subjective realm close to me, gender.

CHAPTER FIVE

Indecent Exposure

REDEFINING THE SPACES
OF GENDER

I want to start this chapter with a piece of advice and a word of caution. Both are directed to women.

First, the advice: perhaps you, like me, have difficulty maintaining your personal space in public areas. Men coming toward you on the sidewalk won't get out of your way. I have found a simple solution: as the man approaches, direct your eyes to his knees and allow a look of casual preoccupation to come over your features. If he refuses to yield right-of-way, direct your vision toward his groin with an air of distracted annoyance. I guarantee he will, sheepishly, veer to his side of the walk.

Perhaps the basis for this tactic's success is that it transforms, in the most unremarkable way, the phallus into the penis. When male social power is revealed to be contingent upon the not especially prepossessing male organ, the psychological force of male power deteriorates. The phallus, as Lacan says, only works when veiled.[1] This tactic compels masculine subjectivity to contract, attach itself to a place with observable physical limits, and cease circulating, like the phallus, in a territory or economy over which it claims unchallenged dominion.

And now a word of caution, for we should not become too bold in testing the powers of the female gaze. When a man looks at you in a clearly predatory way, don't look back. As unpleasant an experience

[1]See Lacan, "The Meaning of the Phallus," in *Feminine Sexuality,* esp. p. 82.

as it is to be subjected to this affront, restrict yourself to the pretense of oblivious object-hood. Don't try to reverse the gaze, to meet him eye to eye in a virtual game of "chicken." Every time I try to deflect the male gaze with a hostile gaze of my own, the man has moved toward me with a visible air of cruelty until I break the connection. It is as if I open up a pathway for physical—rather than simply moral and visual—violation; as if the transverse path opened up between the gazes materializes into a conduit for the conduction of real bodies; as if, by meeting his visual assault, I invite (in his mind) a real penetration.

Perhaps this scenario illustrates another of Lacan's points. Gender is very much a structural relation, the insertion of subjects within an abstract network of preexisting positions. Against Lacan (although he is somewhat against himself on this point), I would suggest that we are *not* free to place ourselves on either side of the sexual divide, as we choose.[2] When the bar is semiotic, maybe; but when the barrier is that diaphanous one dividing the visual field into "mine" and "yours," to play games, to not know one's place, is to open one's self to violent violation, to be reminded that there is a connection between the body and culture, and that culture makes a place for us that often overrides our free choice. No, of course the penis is not the phallus; but in the intricate interrelations that constitute the social field, particularly the unstable fabric of exchanged glances, it might as well be. Markers in language can oscillate supply across the gender line in language, but we, as active social subjects, are stuck in our skin and anchored by it to particular places.

The two scenarios I have presented here mark out the range for my discussion. I will be considering the gaze and its role in establishing relations between subjects that are relations of power, but I will be transferring what I know about the gaze from the cinematic scene to the interpersonal scene where its consequences, though no less the effect of representation, can have more directly physical effects. Examining the legal constitution of an act called "indecent exposure"

---

[2]Actually it may be only his feminist interpreters who want to insist on this point (see, e.g., the statements by Juliet Mitchell and Jacqueline Rose in their introductions to *Feminine Sexuality,* pp. 6 and 48, respectively). As I read Lacan, he is if anything too convincing in demonstrating the cultural determinism at work in forming the sexes; it would, from his account, be almost impossible to vary from the place culture lays out for us on the basis of our sex. Hence the limited role he plays in my own consideration of the production of gender.

will allow me to approach more directly some of the issues that have been gathering throughout the course of this work, namely, How is subjectivity lived as a space by people, and lived differently by different kinds of subjects? When and how do the subjective spaces laid out by discourse, the social environment, and psychic individuation interact, and how can a change in one of these areas—the way we think and write and speak—lead to significant transformations in another: the way we occupy subjectivity? Speaking of the gaze and its power in shaping subjects will also allow me to reground the rather more abstract considerations of poststructural philosophy in a domain closest to me, the everyday struggle of gender, and to see how the two realms—theory and subjective politics—might come into communication to change the everyday life of subjects.

‖

The eyes are, as poets would have it, the "windows on the soul"; they are also, as popular wisdom tells us, our "windows on the world." The eyes are a strange kind of limit, both portal and barrier; like the skin, like consciousness, like the system *Pcpt.–Cs.* described by Freud, they function both to connect me with the world, and to separate me from it. Vision is one of the most crucial sites of subjectivity, and also one of the most anxious: it allows me to see my body as separate from others, while also providing a pathway for the outside world and others in it to invade me and my consciousness. Freud thought it one of the prime instruments of the reality principle, that which constitutes self and other and lets one gauge when an ideation, sensation, or affect originates in the self or when it comes from somewhere/someone else.[3] Undecidably both "inside" and "outside," it acts as a register of the external real and one of the most intimate sites of sensation.

Vision, then, plays a fundamental role in the formation of subjectivity. Lacan considered the visual dichotomy opened up by the mirror stage the foundation of subjectivity.[4] Kaja Silverman adds that we become "subjects" not only in the initial moment when we incor-

---

[3]This thesis is implicit in *Beyond the Pleasure Principle*, and also in *Civilization and Its Discontents*.

[4]Lacan formulates this position in "The Mirror Stage as Formative of the Function I," 1–7.

porate an image (from the mirror) but subsequently when we are "appropriated as image" (161). Subjectivity seems to teeter delicately across that bisection of visual reciprocity: I exist both because I see others and because they see me, literally or metaphorically.

There are warring directions to this balance; when I see outward, my subjectivity has a tendency to expand, to take up the whole world in a form of pure annihilating narcissism. It is only in the returning gaze of the other that I am captured, cut down to size, made to occupy my "proper place." A "healthy" or realistic subjectivity would have to moderate these two tendencies; to be only the image of the other would be to collapse under object-hood, to be crushed under the pressure of an imploding surface. A "realistic self" might, then, oscillate back and forth between annexing too much of the world and conversely owning up to too little. On a similar economy as projection and introjection—but without the suggestion, as in some treatments of that topic, that there is an objectively proper place for the boundary of inside and outside, self and other, to lie—out of the visual dialectic, a self would continually and unceasingly, though always waveringly, be developing. The way vision divides and shapes us synecdochically speaks to the problematics of subjectivity in their entirety. There is no such thing, in any literal or physical sense, as a boundary to the self, and yet the perpetual reinstantiation or reassertion of such a boundary is what serves to establish a self.

Focusing on vision, then, gives us a picture of subjectivity as malleable and negotiable. No wonder "the gaze" has proved to be so fascinating to feminist critics. It promises opportunities both for describing the limits of subjects as they have already been formed and for reconstructing, reshaping subjects. Moreover, the gaze has attracted so much scholarly attention precisely because of the insight it allows on the gender dynamic. Mulvey's landmark work presupposes that vision, depending on whether its subject is a "man" or a "woman," divides space differently. Studies of the gaze have been able to link representation with real divisions of power and to locate both within cultural structures of gender.

Two divergent models of the gaze seem to underlie much feminist writing. The first would see it as a kind of projectile: a thing going out from one subject to another and then being reflected back. This figuration constructs the gaze as a detachable property of subjects who exist, complete and already differentiated, outside the gaze's rebounding trajectory; the gaze moves between but has no effect on subjects who are always-already gendered. The *sex* of the subject looking, and the *sex* of the object looked at, determine the gender dynamics of the gaze.

This way of envisioning the gaze is ultimately defeatist. It outlines a structure of immobility in which we, women, can attain no agency and are destined to perpetual violation. The only recourse, if such an estimation of the gaze and the way it relates gendered subjects is true, is to demand, "Don't look at me!" Evacuating as it does all of the promising ambiguity that turning to the gaze initially offered, this approach hasn't had much currency in feminist analyses, except perhaps in the feminist antiporn movement, whose polemic investments rely, at heart, on assuming an eternal quality to gender identities.

In a second, more Foucauldian figuration, we might see the gaze as a plastic medium, a constitutive field itself forming the power differences between subjects. The direction and quality of the *gaze* determines the gender positionality of the participating *subjects*. In this case, the gaze would be reversible; whoever wields the gaze has power, and thereby turns implicitly "masculine."

This perspective has attracted more attention in feminist thought, as represented, for instance, by Ann Kaplan, who bluntly asks in the title of one essay "Is the Gaze Male?" This approach suggests that our gender, and therefore our relation to power, has nothing to do with the sex of our bodies; it invites me to take on desire and power by simply opening my eyes and daring to see.

However, many feminist critics have hesitated to adopt this position on and in the gaze. If a woman takes on the gaze, does she not simply reverse the binary of gender, leaving its differential structure unaffected, while she indulges in a perverse imitation of masculine omnipotence? Mary Ann Doane argues so: "The male striptease, the gigolo—both inevitably signify the mechanism of reversal itself, constituting themselves as aberrations whose acknowledgement simply reinforces the dominant system of aligning sexual difference with a subject/object dichotomy" (77). In response to the sexualization of stars like John Travolta and Robert Redford, Ann Kaplan offers a pessimistic analysis: reversing the gaze leaves the binary of gender unmoved; it simply reverses positions, putting women where men have traditionally been. The women so positioned take up all the negative qualities associated with masculinity and lose the valuable attributes of femininity, such as "kindness, humaneness, motherliness" (318).

While some feminist film theorists question the desirability of assuming a masculine subject position, I would question instead our practical capacity to simply "change our point of view" in a culture that allocates different points of view to men and women and backs that assignment up with the threat of physical retribution. Encouraging reversal overestimates the agency available to visual partners to transform cultural relations that preexist them. Women are rarely allotted the position of desiring subject, especially in a heterosexual paradigm. Simply deciding to "take" that position can lead to all manner of retribution—from negative representations (as in the recent spate of "reverse sexual harassment" films and novels) to sexual violence (as in "She acted like she wanted it"). I am in agreement with Doane and Kaplan in seeing most examples of masculine sexualization and feminine spectatorship, as they are offered up by popular culture for consumption (e.g., *Playgirl*'s brief heyday in the 1970s) as pure parody, with all the connotations of a lack of seriousness that that term portends.[5] Positions of powerful desire, it sometimes seems, are only offered to women as a joke.

We might begin to wonder whether a reversal of the gendered structure of the gaze is even culturally possible. There is a round-robin equation of looking/power/masculinity—in feminist theory *and* in the larger culture—that I find disturbing. There ought to be some point in the breaks between these three terms to disrupt the perpetual pairing of the gaze with power, and of power with masculinity: Don't we, as feminist critics, wish to gain some of this power for ourselves? Do we want always to name power "masculine," thereby leaving it in men's hands and tautologically distancing it from ourselves? Don't

---

[5]Most of the feminist film critics I've read don't, themselves, take the possibilities of reversal seriously; they focus instead, like the male gaze, on feminine sites, considering the female spectator, once again, only in relation to feminine objects. One example would be Mulvey's own "Afterthoughts on 'Visual Pleasure and the Narrative Cinema,' " which investigates what happens when women look at women rather than what happens when women look at men. To me this move appears masochistic, doubly objectifying, replacing "woman" in the position of object in the very moments when she might become subject, folding her back into the fabric of a gender structure from which we need to escape, preserving the very concentricity of a relation that needs to become bidirectional.

we wish on some level to gain access to the gaze, and the pleasures recumbent in it? Don't we do the work of patriarchy when we endlessly cut ourselves off from power, from the gaze, and locate both in the masculine domain? Isn't feminist theory, finally, not only about describing the ingrained differences between men and women, their subjectivities and capacities and what is socially available to each, but also about changing that differentiation?

To explain the apparent gender solidity of this visual structure, a third and more graphic figuration of the gaze is needed. To my mind, the gaze denotes not an instrument of the already powerful, nor a field open to infinite play, but instead a graphic illustration of what happens when the genders come together. It is an illustration of the complementary shapes drawn for their subjectivities by culture, an indication of the *mutuality* of gender shaping, and a place to test, manipulate, and attempt to reform both the form of the genders and the relation between them. In this depiction, the gaze appears as the middle area in a tripartite space, a flexible boundary taking shape in response to the pressures exerted by either side. The gaze indicates the contours they already possess, but also can be a medium for one side to effect changes in the shape of the other.

I hope it will be no great leap to apply the speculation that film theorists have made about the gazes of cinema to the interactions of people in the three-dimensional space that constitutes the environment of our daily lives; Mulvey begins "Visual Pleasure" by pointing out that the gendered structuration of the gaze in cinema borrows from and reinforces patterns of viewing already established by the larger culture (6). In the landscape of streets, hallways, malls, and parks that map out our everyday existence, a woman may unexpectedly and unwillingly become witness to the spectacle of the naked male body. Investigating what happens between gendered subjects in the case of indecent exposure might reveal quite a bit about the spaces of gender, allowing us to discuss with more complexity the permanence evident in the dynamics of the gaze and finally laying the groundwork for us to conceive remapping the spaces of gender.

— ❖ —

"Flashing," experts agree, is a male crime. The gendered structure of indecent exposure reinscribes itself in discourses on the act, as this statement from criminologist Morris Ploscowe shows: "Neither the ordinary conventions of civilized living nor the penal law permits men to expose their masculinity indiscriminately to any group of passing women and girls" (162). While the offenders may come from any age group and from any educational and social level, they vary little in terms of sex: "It should be noted that indecent exposure is almost exclusively a masculine offense" (Ploscowe 161–162). Their victims are nearly always women or children—about 50% of the victims are under age 16 (Rosen 503). (Ralph Slovenko ventures that this preference for underage victims may result from the fact that they are perceived as less threatening [76]; perhaps the same factor is at work in choosing women.) Some inherent quality of flashing makes it a crime of men against women (and children), both in practice and in ideology. Indecent exposure, the most common of crimes labeled "sexual" (Ploscowe 161), carries the highest rate of recidivism (Slovenko 75).

Such empirical evidence about indecent exposure reflects only the act as it is recorded in arrest and conviction records, and says little about the definition of the act itself; empirical research assumes the fact of the event rather than enquiring into its own terms and exploring what makes certain acts visible as offenses. This sociological approach assumes, in other words, that "indecent exposure" objectively exists, apart from cultural shaping. Investigators go from there to examine the psychological formation of the perpetrators: Why do men commit such acts? The answer to this question generally rests upon suppositions concerning the essential nature of women and men, whether this "nature" is seen as a result of biology or of divergent psychohistories. (Slovenko asserts that the exhibitionist is attempting to reassure himself that he is not castrated. Hence the woman's surprised cry, and even his arrest, are satisfying. They tell him: "I have something to show!" [75].) But I am interested here in concentrating on cultural factors that may be more readily susceptible to intervention. I would like to focus, therefore, not on what leads men to commit this act, but on what leads the female victims to consider it a crime. Certainly flashing is *intended* as an assault, but why is it *received* as one? What cultural and ideological factors might intervene in *perceiving* these acts? It is from a sympathetic and feminine position—a position of desire—rather than from an accusatory (perhaps masculine) position, that I would like to ask, Why can't a woman take pleasure in viewing a man?—even granted that the sight is unexpected.[6] Why, when men are confronted with the nude bodies of women, are they not likewise "assaulted"? The answer to this question will, I believe, lead to a discussion of cultural assumptions and their effect in constructing the subjectivity of men and women so that they become, indeed, different.

To the layman the definition of "flashing" is obvious. Indecent exposure occurs when an individual "exposes his penis and his person in a public place as a means of resolving his own conflicts and problems in relation to sex" (Ploscowe 161). Women may be far less inclined to exhibitionism, even if in film and psychoanalysis, by an "extraordinary sleight of hand," as Kaja Silverman notes, that is the function we have been made to occupy. "Woman" has come to be identified with "narcissism and exhibitionism, which would seem more compatible with male subjectivity—qualities which are almost synonymous with organ display" (Silverman 26). Perhaps women with a proclivity toward exhibitionism redirect their drives through some

[6]Some of my test readers had difficulty grasping the point I am trying to make here, so it might be helpful to clarify—though the point does become clearer as the chapter progresses. Though all positions, including accusatory ones, may be positions of desire, there is a big difference between questions that begin "Why can't I" and "Why can't you." I am attempting, in this sentence, to signify my identification with (heterosexual) women; I wish women, myself among them, could be less defensive in seeking sexual contact. Asking "Why can't women . . . ," without clarifying the positionality of the statement, leaves open the possibility that the speaker is not identifying with women; that the speaker is not interested in what women might want; that the speaker is instead attempting to force women to comply with his desires, in disregard of what women might want. Concerning whether women "can" or "can't" take pleasure in viewing a man, I am simply following up the conclusions suggested by the preceding data: since incidents of males exposing themselves to females were reported as *crimes*, we can assume that these females didn't take pleasure. Expanding the scope to take into account sexual interaction in general, we can assume that women can and do take pleasure in viewing the male body; however, even given the changes wrought by the women's movement, women's experience of sexuality and desire are still much more crisscrossed by contradiction and anxiety than men's. That many women have a *difficult* relation to pleasure, I would state as an established fact; as for the genesis of that difficulty, I would locate it in a continuing tradition of prohibition. If women "can't" take pleasure in being flashed, it is not only because culture tells us not to; it is also because both genders are encouraged to attribute to men the property of sexual agency. We fear that the agency already displayed by the man's act of exposure could proceed to further expressions of agency: to rape. Hence, a woman might have difficulty in enjoying an unexpected glimpse of a man's sex organ because she might fear what comes next. Most men would probably not be afflicted with fear in the same way.

sanctioned behavior, such as nude dancing, and that is why incidents of female flashing are hard to find. Or, perhaps indecent exposure by women lies in a continuum with such sanctioned practices, so that a man confronted with a true act of female "flashing" simply cannot tell the difference. "Flashing" may be obviated in a culture that incites feminine exhibition, and can't perceive it when it occurs. This last is the possibility I find most interesting.

Let's assume that a woman does occasionally confront an unsuspecting man with the shock of her naked flesh. What would explain the legal invisibility of this act? Possibly the man subject to the view may feel—if initially shocked—finally nonplussed and even gratified. Our culture assumes that men want to look at the nude bodies of women and that women do not desire to view the nude bodies of men; that a man's naked body is the sign of aggression and that a woman's exposed flesh is an opportunity for pleasure. While it is now somewhat concealed, this divergence of gender is also inscribed in the New York State Penal Code. What we call "flashing" might fall under the rubric of "Public Lewdness," defined in Article 245.00:

> A person is guilty of public lewdness when he intentionally exposes the private or intimate parts of his body in a lewd manner or commits any other lewd act (a) in a public place, or (b) in a private premises under circumstances in which he may readily be observed from either a public place or from other private premises, and with intent that he be so observed. (*Mckinney's Consolidated Laws* 224)

It might also be classified as an act of "Exposure of a Person":

> A person is guilty of exposure if he appears in a public place in such a manner that the private or intimate parts of his body are unclothed or exposed. For purposes of this section, the private or intimate parts of a female person shall include that portion of the breast which is below the top of the areola. (*Mckinney's Consolidated Laws* 299)

Importantly, however, until 1983, the latter Article 245.01, "Exposure of a Person," was entitled "Exposure of a Female," and was designed to prohibit such practices as topless waitressing and nude dancing. "Public Lewdness" differs from "Exposure of a Person" in that in the former, the portrayal of the genitals in the context of sexual activity, and not simply exposure of the genitals, is paramount (*Mckinney's Consolidated Laws* 297).

It would seem that the law draws a distinction between those crimes capable of being committed by men and others capable of being committed by women. The first law implicitly directs itself toward actions it assumes to be performed by men; the second, toward acts presumed for women. My study of cases prosecuted on the basis of these laws quickly revealed that the gender division implied by the laws holds in the prosecution of different acts. If a man reveals himself in public, his action is *implicitly* lewd and offensive. According to the law, a man's body is inherently sexual and assertive; a woman's is compliant and objectlike. The article on "Exposure of a Person" seems to assume that the woman's body appears passively, through the agency of a purveyor (often masculine). Article 245.01 concerning "Exposure of a Person" continues by excluding from prosecution any woman who exposes her breast when "breast feeding" or while "entertaining or performing in a play, exhibition, show, or entertainment" (*Mckinney's Consolidated Laws* 299). A woman's body opens itself to interpretation: her nudity may be the sign of tender ministrations to her infant—an activity valued by patriarchy, and thereby excusable—or it may be permissible in the context of male pleasure, "entertainment."

Female flashing may be invisible because the laws (and men?) are incapable of interpreting the exposed female body as anything other than entertaining. Even if she should choose nudity for antisocial or political reasons, the woman's body is reincorporated into the circuit of masculine desire. A relevant example can be taken from the case *People v. Harris* from 1972. Rochelle Harris was found "Not Guilty" under article 245.00, pertaining to public lewdness. The *New York Supplement* gives this breathy, disjointed account:

> Where defendant, a woman in her late twenties, removed her bathing suit on public beach and was totally nude, during following one and one-half hours she was observed playing with a ball, swimming, waving at a passing boat, slowly applying suntan lotion (to the frontal portion of her body including her breasts and down to her pubic hair) and sunbathing on a blanket (arms behind her propping her up, legs outstretched and knees approximately 12 to 18 inches apart) and while sunbathing was photographed, actions of defendant, charged with public lewdness, could not be considered lewd beyond a reasonable doubt. (vol. 493, p. 733)

It is as if a woman couldn't get arrested if she *wanted* to, as if her body is implicitly nonaggressive, not actively and intentionally assaultive in a sexual way. The law takes up the side of heterosexual masculinity in viewing the nude female body as a pleasant surprise, a sight it enjoys caressing with its vision (or in this case, its language). But it stands in like a father to protect endangered women from the untoward advances of naked men.

Lewd intentions cannot be attributed to the naked female body, because the female subject is not legally endowed with the agency necessary to formulate such intentions. Laws, and distinctions made within the laws, rely upon assumptions about the differences between male and female sexuality that circulate in the public at large. In the prosecution of flashing, woman, and her desire, turns invisible: whatever intent may be behind her nudity, her nude body becomes an occasion for masculine pleasure.

Likewise, her reaction to viewing nude bodies, male or female, whatever it may be, is erased by the inevitable positioning of her as victim and ward of patriarchal protective mechanisms. Real women, and their individual reactions, become irrelevant in deeming an act of male exposure a crime, because the laws surrounding flashing deem it a social, rather than a personal, offense. Though "flashing" appears in criminology and popular conception alike as the most common of offenses deemed sexual, the law appears oddly imprecise in naming a victim. "Flashing" occupies a marginal place on the edges of several other areas of legal discourse, appearing under a variety of headings in different indexes. In the *United States Supreme Court Digest, 1754 to Date,* it appears as a subset of both obscenity and lewdness, and would seem to be addressable under "sexual assault" or "indecent assault." The definition of "Assault and Battery" in the *United States Supreme Court Digest* includes "acts of violence towards the person of another, either with or without actual touching or striking" (vol. 3 s Ct D11). But New York State reserves the title "Sex Offenses" for instances of *physical contact,* which visual contact apparently is not.

Morton Enelow notes that the law often treats exhibitionism and voyeurism under the same heading, "Creating a Public Nuisance" (479). It would be important to distinguish, I would think, between cases of generalized exposure (e.g., the drunken "streaking" of a fraternity group, or public nudity in the service of political protest) and that directed toward a specific individual or individuals: the first is a public act, the second is interpersonal. But the laws do not necessarily make those distinctions. Thus homosexual activity in a public toilet, a rowdy orgy in a (deserted) public building, and even the copulation of a bull and cow too near a public road "within the sight and presence of women and children" (Ploscowe 158) were prosecuted under the heading of "Lewdness," under which indecent exposure may also be classified. Other authors treat indecent exposure as "Obscenity," a classification mostly otherwise concerned with obscene publications, pictures, and advertising. However, indecent exposure, like obscene language (another unexpected subset of "Obscenity"), escapes the realm of the commercial and economic, and refers to a battle of desires or wills taking place on an interpersonal level.

The law marginalizes women a second time by calling indecent exposure an assault against "community standards," rather than individual persons. The act of indecent exposure is, in some ways, not an assault on an individual at all: instead, it is a crime because it offends the disembodied person of "the community." This conflation tends to conceal the sexuality at work in acts of (and the legal act of constituting an area called) "Indecent Exposure." Since the recipients of the unwelcome sight of "indecent exposure" proper are almost always women and children, calling the act an "Offense against Public Sensibilities" conceals the particular qualities of the subjects chosen for the offense. It is as if the startled victim is taken only as a miniature replica of, a fragmentary example of, "the general public," the *real* addressee of the act.

However, I would argue that the crimes seem continuous not because it is thought that the victim represents a small example of public standards. The two are continuous because "public standards" are thought to reflect, and brought in to protect, the consciousnesses and consciences of women and children—as the judgment concerning publicly copulating animals makes very clear. A woman's desire, her agency, and her subjectivity are thereby twice elided. Real women and their reactions are replaced by imaginary (perhaps ideal) women and their presumed (or perhaps expected or required) reactions.

A woman can be arrested for indecent exposure, it would seem, only when her actions victimize the femininely defined personage "the public," which, including children, is assumed to have even less power and to be in even greater need of protection than she. As Alexander Smith and Harriet Pollack point out, the activities of prostitutes in soliciting customers often embarrass or offend the individual men they approach. However, cases are normally brought against these women not because of their effect on a vulnerable male client, but because they have become so extreme, collectively, as to offend and disrupt the community (120). Nude dancing, public displays of pornography, and nearly all cases in which the female body prominently appears in cultural view, are "victimless" crimes, which become criminal only when they assault standards of public decency. Only women and children—not men—can be made victims of indecent exposure.

Indecent exposure, like rape, is a deed for which men are arrested and in which women and girls are the victims. By blending the person with the populace, the penal code camouflages the sexual specificity of the crime, the fact that it *is* a sexual offense, an act of power and desire that is not reciprocated. "Flashing" is meant to be an assault, and it is received as one by the woman so assaulted. I do not wish to erase the presence of women a third time, by saying that flashing does not exist, or that it is not an assault. Nor would I propose the eradication of laws that attempt to protect women from these kinds of daily violation. Such laws are necessary to mediate the cultural interaction of subjects who currently exist in an environment saturated with systemic imbalances of power (and other properties). However, I would argue that the structure of this act—discursively and in reality—takes its form from the ways in which gendered subjects are constituted—discursively and in reality—and that the shapes that gendered subjectivity takes are historically specific.

In our current cultural moment, femininity—discursive, psychological, and real—appears to be almost synonymous with violation. The popular conception of indecent exposure interprets the act as a "psychic rape," a lesser but similar form of sexual violation.[7] Like

---

[7]Comparing flashing and rape is understandable because both take place in an already established dichotomy of the sexes that results in real inequalities of power. Both depend upon preconceptions about the nature of the sexes that determine not only the definition of an act as a crime, but, very possibly, determine the fact that the crime occurs. That is, the ideological differentiation of the sexes may cause men to assault women, just as it causes women and society at large to define certain acts as assaults. English common law defines rape as the "illicit carnal knowledge of a female by force and against her will." As Judith Baer clarifies in her contribution to the *Encyclopedia of the American Justice System,* vol. 3, pp. 1252–1270, this cast to rape laws means that "traditionally, a male can not be raped, although in reality he can be forcibly sodomized; nor can a female rape, although in reality she can sexually abuse anyone whom she can subdue. (These acts are sometimes punishable, however, as sodomy or assault)" (1265). The definition of rape filters inherent attributes of a violent act through broad cultural assumptions about gender identity (and a heterosexist bias). Even should a woman rape a man—with a prosthesis or with her vagina (?!)—it cannot be considered rape. A woman is not, by definition, capable of taking an active or violent sexual role. If she does perform an action that exhibits the qualities of rape, she commits an "assault"—her action is *not* sexual.

rape, exhibitionism is something that men do to women, but that women may never do to men. In the case of rape, the penis forcibly enters the vulva or another bodily orifice (anus, mouth). In the case of indecent exposure, the penis forcibly enters the woman's consciousness, through the passive portal of her vision.[8] Her vision is submissive—she cannot control or stop it—and, as if it were a tunnel or pathway akin to a metaphorical vagina, it provides the route for her violation. She cannot possess her gaze with power or for her own pleasure. It is as if men's and women's visual faculties are constituted homologously to their bodies, or specifically, to their sexual organs. It is as if a man's body, even as a passive spectacle, cannot function except in aggressive penetration, a woman's vision except as receptacle. In flashing, the customary subject–object relation of men and women analyzed by feminist film theorists under the rubric of "the gaze" is almost exactly reversed, and yet the power relation remains unchanged.

Men are arrested for assaulting children, women, and the public; women are arrested for offending children and the public. Small children are never arrested for indecent exposure (even though theirs are the kind of bodies one most frequently sees nude). This implies a hierarchical arrangement of subjects from man through woman to child, in an ascending capacity for sexual activity and a contrasting and descending capacity for moral and psychological fortitude. The law is only resting on a broader cultural ideology in assuming that subjectivity is something like a container, measurably open or closed.

The violation that makes indecent exposure a criminal act is a violation of consciousness, emotional rather than physical in nature; as Ploscowe notes, the victim may be "seriously frightened" (162). "Serious fright" implies psychic damage. That such damage is thought

---

[8]Comparing rape and indecent exposure is understandable, but also unwarranted, because flashing is not physical and violent in the same way. Many authors take care to point out that exhibitionism is a complete act in itself and not a preface to further violation. Ismond Rosen tells us that it is rare for instances of exposure to proceed to violence; the very fact that they are performed in such obviously public areas indicates that no further contact—no seduction or attempt at rape—is imminent. Ploscowe too attests that "fortunately, the exhibitionist is not generally a dangerous individual. His sexual behavior will not go beyond exposure. He normally does not attempt to lay a hand on any of his victims. . . . He may seriously frighten his victims, but he will not attempt to injure them physically" (162). Even though common sense tells us that flashing does not proceed rape, we nonetheless receive it as a quasi-physical assault.

to be (and indeed may be experienced as) "damage" sufficiently significant to deem flashing a crime, on top of the fact that it is a crime almost wholly committed against women and girls, implies two things: one, that some kind of comparison exists between physical and psychic damage, and two, that women's psyches appear particularly susceptible to such harm. Independently of Freud (though both rely on commonplace suppositions), in the legal view the psyche appears, like the body, to be protected by a skin or envelope that can, through trauma—as the body can through force—be ruptured.[9] We, women, just as much as the law, perceive ourselves to be vulnerable and in need of a legal shield that will take the place of the "natural" psychic shield men possess. Hence our cultural location becomes embodied in a psychological attitude, a psychic constitution. The reception of indecent exposure is one place where the borders of psyche and body forcibly coincide; when the perpetrator plans the act, no doubt the symbolic outline of "woman" comes into play as a determining factor as well.

Following these observations, one could propose that men and women occupy and are effected not just by divergent physical spaces—bodies—or by social positioning, but also exhibit distinctive and different psychological formations, or psychic spaces. Our interior worlds, the shape of our consciousnesses, exhibit qualitatively divergent shapes. Gender ideology, it could be pointed out, not only determines our interactions in space, but defines us *as* space. "Woman" connotes a space that is penetrable, susceptible, passive, submissive, imploding, collapsing in upon itself; "man" derives from a space assumed to be expansive, rigid, and intrusive.

—·—✳✦✳—·—

It is not only law and the discourses of other presumably masculinist institutions that make these assumptions about the texture of gendered consciousness. Feminist psychoanalytic literature likewise assigns a distinctive spatial quality to feminine being. I will take only two examples, from very different traditions.

Nancy Chodorow's *The Reproduction of Mothering: Psychoanalysis and the Sociology of Gender* contends that male and female infants come to be "masculine" or "feminine" subjects, men and women, by assuming

---

[9]The most relevant Freudian text on this subject is *Beyond the Pleasure Principle*.

quite different psychic attitudes in relation to the mother, and eventually in relation to others in general. She suggests that what makes men and women different is a disparity in our psychic spaces. We receive our subjective constitutions in complement to the psychic space provided us by our mothers. The psychic surroundings of male children will be marked by boundaries and separations. For girls, the milieu will carry qualities of fusion and proximity. The maternal ideation of the mother—her creation of a certain kind of unbounded space for the female child—will be successfully picked up by the little girl as part of her own psychic structure, not by identification, but because the indeterminacy of the mother's psychic edges leaves the child's own limits indeterminate. The girl's subjective boundary is better figured as a fuzzy gray area, where the other and the one meet and mingle with each other, than as the neat black slash thought to compose the traditional individual.

The female mother sees the male infant as different from herself and sets up, in her actions and in her mind, a much deeper schism between herself and her male child. The boy internalizes this "otherness," the idea of himself as other, and turns the attitude backward: for the male child, individuality is predicated on a rigid autonomy and repudiation of the other: the mother, the feminine. Implicit (cf. 167) in Chodorow's argument is the sense that boys, by renouncing femininity and their original constitution in an interwoven relationship to another, are to an extent subject to (and subjects by) a fiction. Their psyches feature an unyielding surface and an incapacity to be open to the advances of others.

Chodorow succinctly summarizes the generative effects of this differing maternal treatment: "Because of their mothering by women, girls come to experience themselves as less separate than boys, as having more permeable ego boundaries. Girls come to define themselves more in relation to others" (88).[10]

Luce Irigaray describes "woman's" condition in ways similar to

---

[10]It might be wise to refine Chodorow's thesis, however, before applying it to materially existing persons: rather than differentiating between "men's" and "women's" subjective attitudes, we might differentiate between a "masculine" and a "feminine" psychic texture. Women can take up a rigidly bounded psychic position, just as men might display a porous or sensitized ego surface. One of the interesting features of flashing is how it seems to cause the individual ego to coincide with the "appropriate" subjective format laid out by gender.

Chodorow's, but in the totally different context of French poststructuralism. She leaves the distinction between the symbolic or metaphysical category of "the feminine" and the empirical class "women" undefined. To Irigaray, "woman" is a being of diffuse nature, the penultimate example of that which disrupts boundaries, unsettles borders, and throws into crisis the certitude of phallogocentric unity. To illustrate the difference in the space of femininity, Irigaray's well-known essay employs the figure of woman's sex, the "sex which is not one," the vulva, whose slippery dual lips cannot quite be separated or located, themselves, or pinpointed as inferior or superior to the clitoris.

The culmination of her drive toward (re)defining woman's space is reached, in *This Sex,* in the essay "The 'Mechanics' of Fluids," where she argues that femininity resembles a liquid. Irigaray uses the assumptions and blindnesses of science as a token for the biases of masculine systems of knowledge and representation as a whole. Fluids, for science, have been untheorized and invisible, just as femininity has been for psychoanalysis. Fluids and femininity are *"in excess with respect to form"* and therefore *"rejected as beneath or beyond the system currently in force"* (110, italics in original). Femininity, that which defies enclosure and closure, partitioning and autonomy, is boundaryless, and women's psychic processes have been inaccessible to psychoanalysis precisely because they follow this different physics, whereas both the physical sciences and the "science" of psychoanalysis are based on logics of enumeration, visibility, and identity. Femininity registers a space that is (to quote from "The 'Mechanics' of Fluids") "continuous, compressible, dilatable, viscous, conductible, diffusible"; "unending, potent and impotent owing to its resistance to the countable"; that "enjoys and suffers from a greater sensitivity to pressures"; that "allows itself to be easily traversed by flow by virtue of its conductivity to currents coming from other fluids or exerting pressure through the walls of a solid"; that "mixes with bodies of a like state, sometimes dilutes itself in them in an almost homogeneous manner, which makes the distinction between the one and the other problematic"; that is "already diffuse 'in itself,' which disconcerts any attempt at static identifications" (Irigaray 111).

Both Chodorow and Irigaray, then, attribute to women the same psychic qualities attributed to women in the legal discourse surrounding sex crime: receptiveness, porousness, softness, susceptibility. The definition of indecent exposure rests on broad cultural assumptions about gender identity that are no less foundational to a lot of theory.

I am convinced that the theory, like the law, documents truths about the nature of gendered subjectivity as it exists at this point in history. Both feminist theorists seem to be indicating that the positioning of women by masculine cultural and ideological systems has effected a real difference in the consistency of the feminine psyche. Masculine and feminine psyches, derivatives of disparate yet complementary kinds of spaces, occasionally come together in ways that forcibly reinscribe the most gender-typical outlines for their subjectivities; but more than that, indecent exposure, as a shock and offense, is only possible as a result of the differential gender formations that already exist. These disparate psychic attitudes seem to act as something like a default mode that individual men and women can test to varying extents, but that seem too to be powerful shapers of gender interaction and experience. Supposing a divergence in psychic consistency helps to explain the permanence and solidity of gender differences such as that evident in the unequal visual relations of the gaze.

While both Chodorow and Irigaray, to very different ends, make an asset of the pour-ousness or liquidity of feminine identity, its malleability, the analysis of indecent exposure suggests that this form for femininity enables the daily violations we as women experience. My final question is whether the shape given to feminine consciousness is one that we want to perpetuate, whether the space of "woman" is one that we want to continue to occupy. Do we want to maintain this susceptibility on the part of the feminine subject, or do we want to find ways to bolster our defenses?

Most feminist critics would seek to render changes in the shape of gender personalities and the forms of relation possible between the sexes. Chodorow and Irigaray are among them; Chodorow finds merit in the psychic structure of femininity only to recommend transforming *masculinity*, so that it too can attain characteristically "feminine" openness and softness.[11] Irigaray, while validating the structural fluidity

---

[11]I believe that the political potential of Chodorow's work has often been underestimated by other feminist critics. Like the poststructuralists discussed in the previous chapter, Chodorow seeks to change the political structure by shifting the bounds of subjects. She sees the subject not as a self-enclosed, complete, and autonomous entity, but as the effect of a partnering. The (nascent) subject assumes the shape projected for it by another (the mother). Chodorow sees, then, transforming

of the feminine, does so to achieve a polemic, theoretical, and psychological solidity—even rigidity—that will separate "woman" from patriarchal designs.

Disturbing the gaze's symmetry may be one way to disturb the smooth reproduction of gender identities. If, as Jacqueline Rose writes in the provocatively titled "Sexuality in the Field of Vision," "a confusion at the level of sexuality brings with it a disturbance of the visual field" (226), then perhaps the effect of stabilized gender is created in part by the parceling and arrangement of the visual field. Perhaps we need to reverse Rose's formula: disturbing the set markers of the visual field may be one way to disrupt—to confuse—to reorganize—the smooth (re)production of sexuality and sexual positioning. In *Alice Doesn't,* Teresa de Lauretis attempts to study film as a site where "the masculine–feminine polarity can be disrupted to open other spaces for identification, other positionalities of desire" (83) beyond reversal or reinscription. De Lauretis proposes setting up alternative or third positions, to subvert the structure of the visual binary that situates some subjects as powerful masters of violable objects, and does so along lines well worn by the gender arrangement of our culture. Changing the effect of the gaze would, then, entail reconfiguring subjective space, distorting the customary composition of the seeing subject in relation to space.

Poststructuralist critics examined in the preceding chapter advocated similar transformations, but did so using psychosis as their paradigm. I would propose that the kinds of reconstructions of identity being recommended by the above feminists are already happening, and happen all the time. Subjectivity—including gender subjectivity, psychoanalysis tells us—is initially shaped largely by interpersonal, familial relations during infancy and early childhood. As the preceding discussion should have shown, however, it is effected too by ideological interpellation, interpersonal relationships on an adult scale, and the influence of discourse. Changes in discourse can and should be able

---

family relations as the route to redefining subjects and larger social change. But because of her emphasis on intersubjectivity, Chodorow also leaves open the possibility that reconfigurations of the subject could occur through pressures exerted by social partners on adult subjects. It is this kind of reconfiguration I am attempting to portray, and recommend, in this chapter.

to influence the shape of subjectivity. To illustrate this potential, I will
now turn to another representation, one that might appear far removed
from the lofty concerns of academic theory, but that connects back
with it through the body of feminism.

Indecent exposure isn't much studied anymore in criminology.
Perhaps the naked male body as a site for feminine anxiety is beginning
to disappear in law as well as in culture. One of the main forces
underlying such a shift, if it has occurred, would have to be the advance
of feminism and its popular front, the women's movement, which
have given us the capacity to occupy positions of desire and power,
reforming the feminine psyche so that it can be something other than
a space of continual implosion. There would seem to be a long distance
between reclaiming a space for "Woman" in discourse and reforming
the space of the feminine psyche, but I would like to propose otherwise.

Chodorow and Irigaray represent the aim of contemporary feminism to give women a space of resistance. While making of Woman
a transient and fleeting space, each is seeking to provide for real
women, for feminism, a space of considerable fortitude. In the gendered binary of subjective constitutions our culture has arranged, Man
appears as a dilating space, expanding his frontiers ever outward, and
Woman as a cringing, shrinking space forever vulnerable to his attack.
Irigaray suggests a third position: a rigid, bounded space that neither
recedes nor attacks. This, as Diana Fuss has argued, has been the project
of many French (and other) feminists so often accused of essentialism:
a strategic, not an ontological, move. They "define" Woman not to
draw up prescriptions for what women are and should be, but to offer
a location, a standpoint, for resistance; not to say what she is, but to
say *that* she is. If Woman has for so long been little more than the
circle of light projected by a masculinist culture, we need to assert
that Woman *is*—different; take back some of the territory ceded to
masculine inscription, not necessarily to fill it in or people it with
qualities of our own choosing, but simply to leave it a blank outline
that is, nonetheless, a space of our own. Each theorist provides a model
for shifting the cultural landscape and the location of women within

it. Feminism, regardless of how it may reinscribe the conventional "softness" of women, also offers women a position of resistance that has changed not only the way everyday women live their spaces, but also the very psyche that they live as space.

The scene with which I would like to conclude demonstrates how the discourse of feminism has indeed provided for feminine consciousness a space from which to react, or act, differently. The scene comes from the opening credit sequence of the now-defunct but feminist-acclaimed television show "Cagney and Lacey."

Younger readers and TV-phobics might appreciate a brief synopsis of the series. "Cagney and Lacey" ran through most of the 1980s on CBS. It was a dramatic series following the personal and professional lives of two women who became partners and detectives in the New York City Police Department. Christine Cagney, the younger partner, was conventionally attractive and sexually active; the show took up such serious issues as her relationship with her alcoholic father, her own struggles with alcoholism, her decision to have an abortion, the repercussions of date rape. The older partner, Marybeth Lacey, had a semiemployed husband, two young sons, and eventually an infant daughter; the program followed her ongoing struggles to balance work and family, her husband's needs and her own. What distinguished this program from so many imitators was its seriousness. It treated its two main characters with a warmth, humanity, and dignity not often accorded women on prime-time television.

As the opening credit sequence rolls, we see shots of Cagney jogging and purchasing a hot dog, Lacey pointing a gun and greeting her husband. Each of these shots seems to locate Cagney and Lacey in positions alternately phallic and feminine; we are shown that they can occupy places traditionally masculine and traditionally feminine, vacillate across the gender divide, and even actively (one could interpret) undermine or destroy the phallus. But the scene I want to focus on does neither.

The shot is brief: Cagney and Lacey, smiling, are walking toward us down a crowded city sidewalk, each holding the arm of a man who walks between them. In the foreground, his back to us, is another man wearing (stereotypically) a raincoat. As they come abreast of him, he opens it, presumably displaying his genitals. Cagney and Lacey do not squawk; they do not arrest him. They offer responses that are neither stereotypically masculine nor feminine. Cagney looks the man in the groin, and then in the face, and then looks away. She has refused to be penetrated by the sight.

Now, this scene is only a representation, and does not guarantee that non-TV characters who are women would have the capacity to be likewise nonchalant. And yet, I would argue, the possibility of this reaction becoming representable symptomatizes a larger change in the symbolic configuration of "Woman," at the same time that it reinforces that reconfiguration, allowing female viewers to imagine themselves differently.[12] The scene from "Cagney and Lacey" offers a new positionality to women that exists not only as positionality, but that confers a new consistency for feminine subjectivity in relation. The transaction taking place in this scenario neither maintains Woman in her traditional position as object nor catapults her into the place of aggressing subject. It is no mere reversal, but a third option: Woman maintains a place in the visual dichotomy, but forges her own space, one not immediately inundated or swallowed by the masculine sector. The reaction of Cagney documents and enables a new physics for the feminine psyche, and from this avenue—popular culture, just as the most esoteric of French feminist theory—we can see how transforming the form of femininity in discourse can transform the form of feminine subjectivity as it is lived.

As Foucault has argued, power is a relation and the outcome of negotiation. As he has also argued, institutions and discourses produce subjects at the same time that they produce and reproduce power relations. We cannot "think" our way out of oppression by pretending it doesn't exist. Nor, when we are faced with the most obviously repressive and aggressive acts of power, should we "lay back and enjoy it." But, as much as possible, we need to distinguish between instances

---

[12]My project here could be described as an attempt to reclaim or use differently the raw material of concrete space. Derek Gregory (in *Geographical Imaginations*) reminds me that Henri Lefebvre also saw revolutionary promise in the reclamation and reformation of concrete space; Gregory refers to Lefebvre in viewing concrete space as "the site of resistance and active struggle, the origin of spaces of representation that provide counterdiscourses and create alternative spatial imaginaries" (405). Lefebvre sets up concrete space, material space, as primary in the hierarchy of potential spaces. Being basically an Althusserian, I tend conversely to see the various forms of space (representational, abstract, concrete) as much more mutually influential, and would give discourse considerable credit for its ability to influence the design of concrete space and the interaction of bodies/subjectivities within it.

in which power is simply imposed and instances that offer us choices and a variety of responses. In the "space of play" provided by representation, there lies room for renegotiating the psychic and ideological boundaries of subjectivity. If power is, at least in some situations, the result of an unequal or asymmetrical spatial layout—as seems to be the case with the gaze—then what is called for is a reformation of those spatial parameters. The discourse of contemporary feminism has redrawn the boundaries of gender, and offered to women a site of power not analogous to masculine aggression, but truly a site of resistance.

CONCLUSION

Re: Shaping Subjectivity

Space would seem to provide the ideal material for linking the many dimensions of the subject that have interested critics. It brings together the physical space of bodies and their circulation in man–made terrains with the configuration of social categories and the shaping forces of representation. Thus it is an appealing medium for inscribing subjectivity, in all its complexity: for linking together its many dimensions and the theories that concern them.

Griselda Pollock's *Vision and Differences* provides one example of a study that attempts such an application of space, and as such provides a final opportunity for mapping out the work that still remains. Her chapter on modernity and gender links the gendered layout of the gaze, the sexual division of social spaces (rooms, houses, and public areas), and the differences in compositional strategies of men and women painters. Her analysis draws connections "not only [between] the spaces represented, or the spaces *of* representation, but the social spaces from which the representation is made and its reciprocal positionalities" (66). She considers the possibility of seeing "femininity" as a space created in and disseminated by social practice:

> The spaces of femininity are those from which femininity is lived as a positionality in discourse and social practice. They are the product of a lived sense of social locatedness, mobility and visibility, in the social relations of seeing and being seen. Shaped within the sexual politics of looking they demarcate a particular social organization of the gaze which itself works back to secure a particular social ordering of sexual differences. Femininity is both the condition and the effect. (66)

146

I find Pollock's approach intriguing for the way it "grounds" femininity, linking together the construction of gender positions in discourse, the arrangement of built space, and the composition of subjects within social relations. This passage gives substance to "femininity," seeing it not just as an abstract term of discourse but as a physical structure that subjects occupy and that opens them up as an interiority to live. But Pollock stops just short of extending her analysis to a fourth dimension, that of the psyche. In a note she adds:

> In earlier drafts of this chapter I explore the possibilities of co-ordinating the historical perspectives on the spaces of modernity and femininity with those of feminist psychoanalytical writing on femininity (Cixous, Irigaray and Montrelay) between which there was tantalizing coincidence on the issues of the look, the body and the tropes of distance and proximity in the construction and feminine negotiation of sexual difference under a patriarchical system. The use of a statement by Luce Irigaray as introit, and the citation from Mary Kelly, marks the possibility of that reading which could not be undertaken here without massively enlarging this chapter. (87)

I share the trepidation that I perceive underlying Pollock's note. The correspondence between social divisions of space and the possibility of defining a gendered division of psychic space leads into an area both threatening and exciting. To link them too closely is to risk essentialism: feminist criticism has struggled for the last three decades to dismantle the idea that there are inherently "male" and "female" personalities. Proposing gender-differentiated psychologies seems to lead right back into that nature-based explanation for gender differences, especially when—as I am—one is speaking of gender-differentiated psychic *structures*. Somehow the idea of a structure—which sounds so material, so three-dimensional—seems to imply that we're talking about physical structures, such as the brain. Implying such a basis for gender differentiation could not be farther from my intention.

The possibility of drawing correlations between external space and internal space—while threatening because it is so potentially simplifying—is also exciting because it reintroduces a dimension too frequently lost these days in feminist and other kinds of critical theory: the understanding of the experience of gender; the way that the individual occupies a subjective category such as gender; and how a social, ideological, or discursive category shapes subjectivity, both consciousness of self and ways of perceiving others, to such an extent that the subject itself becomes a "space" capable of being analyzed in articulation with the others.

One end that I hope this work has accomplished is to introduce the "space of the subject" as an interpretive category. At this point, I am using the phrase not as a general description of the various ways subjectivity might be plotted, or of the various places that subjects appear, but in a more specific sense: to describe the very *structure* of subjectivity, the space of the individual consciousness, psychic space. While many critics have employed (if not always self-consciously) the language of geography while considering issues of ethnicity and nationality, or the layout of built space while considering the social placement of subjects, few outside of psychology (particularly object relations psychology) have fully considered the possibility of taking subjectivity—consciousness, the experience of being a subject—as an aspect of the subject capable of being described in terms of space. Many are not taking that aspect of subjectivity into account at all (Pollock shies away from it in the passages reprinted above; we saw Mohanty progressively distance herself from it in the work from her covered in Chapter One). It ought to be possible to coordinate all the "spaces of the subject" and examine, finally, how all of the other spaces—for example, social, physical, geographical, and semiotic—link up to the constitution of particular subjectivities: the texture of consciousness and how it is lived, what forms of relating are available to it, what is its likelihood of seeking power, its capacities for receptiveness and change. We bring with us to each relation a provisional shape that tends to shape in turn the relationship; at the same time, all forms of interaction also recursively shape the self. Hence in speaking of subjective structures, I am not in any way relying on notions of inherent or inborn psychological attitudes, but on a notion of the subject as malleable and open to reformation. The "space" of subjectivity—the shape it takes in relation—has to do with modes of interaction; and these sorts of behaviors, though often partially learned from familial interaction, are socially formed through and through. Moreover, we learn and relearn them throughout life; indeed, appropriate modes may change dramatically as we move through different social situations, between contrasting groups, or up or down the scale of cultural privilege.

Incorporating the space of subjectivity provides a new analytic category that reveals perhaps previously hidden aspects of our culture, particularly power relations and their capacities for shaping subjects involved in them. History shows us that forms of consciousness are historically variable; it can at least be hypothesized, for instance, that not only the concept but also the experience of subjectivity was different in 1600 than in 1900; that the intermittent, fluid subject in crisis theorized by Freud did not become possible, in a certain form, until the modern period; and that the fortified, autonomous subject envisioned by Enlightenment thinkers may be fading away. Likewise it can at least be hypothesized that forms of consciousness vary from culture to culture, from nation to nation, and from group to group. Members of particular groups, defined by race or sex boundaries, may have divergent subjective structures, not only because of their participation in a subculture that may promote alternate concepts of selfhood and identity, but also because of their differential positioning in relation to the cultural dominant; in their physical, personal, and professional mobility; and in regard to cultural and social attitudes projected toward them.

It was Freud who pointed out that the ego, the function "I," took its form as something like an accretion of the physical outlines of the body. If this is so, then it must result from the way that body is perceived by others, taken as a guide for how that individual is to be treated by other individuals and cultural processes at large, what place the owner (or subject) of that body takes in the larger field of social relations. Analyzing the shape of that subjectivity, then, opens up new directions for examining our culture, and evaluating (and critiquing) the way it shapes its subjects—nourishing and fortifying some, warping and stunting others. (While I do not hold masculine, or Enlightenment, autonomy as the standard for human subjectivity, it is indicative that our *culture* does so—and that it tends to confer this form of selfhood on men.)

We need to gain a further understanding of the ways in which discursive categories such as race or sexual orientation affect not just the *contents* of someone's mind, but the very forms her or his consciousness, her or his personality, is able to take. I might guess that persons deemed "other" by our culture are intimately familiar with the play of surfaces and borders that Fredric Jameson describes; that the heightened awareness attached to our physical surfaces—our skin, our "looks"—leads frequently enough to an obsessive attention to our own ego boundaries that causes self-consciousness, anxiety, and sensitivity to become primary psychological modes. Just as much, we need to understand what familial, social, or geographical factors might intervene in making such a generalization impossible. One direction my research might lead, then, is toward an analysis of subjective structures, of differential phenomenologies, and their relation to cultural positioning. Perhaps this study will find literary–critical application after all.

   The other advance I hope this work might have made comes strictly in the domain of cultural criticism. I hope it will have laid the foundation for a more subtle and supple articulation of the various dimensions of subjectivity. The point is to write the subject back into studies of subjectivity, to remap the subject into all of these domains, without getting fixed in any one domain, incapable of seeing over the fences between them. Space provides precisely the substance we have been looking for to provide a multidimensional analysis of subjectivity, one that can be truly material without losing sight of the vitality of the inner life of individual subjects, that can incorporate "experience" into broader categories such as global economic relations, while maintaining the flexibility and the fluidity for imagining ways of transforming future subjects. I wish to conclude by proposing a new concept for theorizing subjectivity, one that articulates all of the spaces I have been treating in this work, one that brings them together and coordinates them without arresting them or arresting the transformative potential of (postmodern) subjects. I borrow from a field only occasionally familiar to most literary and cultural critics, and perhaps less so in geography: object relations psychoanalysis, and in particular D. W. Winnicott's concept of "space of play." The ways in which I wish to use Winnicott's phrase move beyond his original intentions, but the phrase itself captures beautifully not only the spatiality I have been attempting to incorporate into my approaches to the subject, but also the elasticity, the revisability that remain when we conceive of the subject as the effect of a provisional boundary that is continually being sketched back into existence. Winnicott's theory might be supplemented by similar approaches, like that embodied in Kristeva's thought on "abjection," which provide more emphasis on textuality and the role of language in underwriting or parsing out personalities, but for the time being I would prefer Winnicott's method: his emphasis on reality over textuality and on the materializing effects of our own self-concepts.

Sketched out in *Playing and Reality*, the "space of play" belongs neither to subject nor to reality, but functions to keep those two areas separate. According to Winnicott, the space of play exists "as a resting-place for the individual engaged in the perpetual human task of keeping inner and outer reality separate yet interrelated" (2). It arises in late infancy as the baby first begins to negotiate the difference between psychic and objective reality. In this sense it resembles Freud's system *Pcpt.–Cs.* It is the suture—both bond and separation—between subject and world that is maintained throughout life to become the space allowing meaningful and rich experience. It is both the blurring that allows the self to engage in and be shaped by the world, and the frail boundary that allows the self to persist. The physics of this space remind us of but surpass in complexity the "in-difference" of the spaces listed by the poststructuralist theorists of Chapter Four (or in some cases, it seems to represent what they were looking for but could not quite name). The space of play envelopes, and thereby creates, a subject whose reality is a continual negotiation with an external or objective reality; the subject is connected to, but might also deviate from, this reality; but more importantly, this subject, because it is constituted by this space of negotiation and revision, is seen as subject to a continual process of re-creation.

However, Winnicott's space of play is not to be found solely in that interstitial space at the midpoint between subject and reality, which reality testing is supposed to concretize and which imagination tests. While in part the shadow of that line (which common sense, and Freud, cannot help but suppose has an objective, proper place), the space of play seems to suggest a third space, not the property of either subject or reality, one that, because it is the place where such distinctions get made, cannot be incorporated, "located," in either. The space of play signifies the zone of play surrounding, delimiting, the subject, but it also signifies another space outside: the external environment where the subject plays. No doubt Winnicott coined this phrase to suggest not only the psychic envelope, but also the rooms full of toys, other objects, and people that exist apart from the infant, but that need the playing infant to activate them, and that exist precisely for the infant subject to activate. It suggests the social atmosphere where we all interact, the physical environment where subjects encounter one another, and may be transformed by the experience.

The space of play mutates, in a later chapter, into the "place of cultural location." The transitional space separates and relates inner and outer reality, but also subject and *subject*. Other subjects are not made into objects, to which one relates as if to books or trees, but retain their character as "other," endowed with the same interiority one supposes for the self. I find Winnicott's depiction of object relations richer than that of many other authors (significantly, Freud) because he does not convert other subjects into objects, or assume that the subject does so, making them the recalcitrant material of narcissistic drives. The transitional space holds the whole social field together, relating subjects to each other and to reality, but maintaining between them a certain amount of slack, room for maneuvering, a certain space for "play" or reconfiguration. Winnicott's transposition of the space of play, a subjective field, onto the larger cultural field, reminds us too of the linkage between our interpersonal interaction and the forms of relationship laid out by discourse and larger cultural representation; of the way that culture maps out patterns for our interaction, and the way real interpersonal contact can replicate, deviate from, and finally modify those discourses—and vice versa.

Winnicott's phrase can be adapted to name what I am trying to get at in attempting to imagine how writing, how theory, can remold the spaces of the subject, the spaces of gender. The space of play can denote the limits of individual subjects and the often tense bond between them, but it can also refer to the broader field of cultural representation in which we are all situated, that itself is responsible for drawing the appropriate lines, and to which we all (to varying degrees) have access. As much as the social field is a place where subjects come together, interact, and occasionally leave transformed, the semiotic field is a place where boundaries get drawn, erased, shifted, and reinscribed. While once the intermediary space that formed us as egos was located on the familial and strictly interpersonal scale, as we become social actors, we are launched into relations whose form will be orchestrated as often by cultural and discursive factors as by interpersonal contact. I am not suggesting that these forces surpass our capacities for intervention; actually, I believe that we maintain access to them through the connective thread of representation, which, like the transitional space (and perhaps in the context of the individual in culture, the two are precisely the same) rests both undecidably "inside" and "outside" the subject, and functions to determine their difference. Language, then, is our umbilicus, giving us life in the social field and forming the capillary of interchange with the social field, thereby allowing us a reverse influence. My suggestion is that the two fields— social and discursive—should be seen as juxtaposed surfaces. A reading of subjective rearticulation could coordinate these two spaces, and examine how compositional effects in one arena transfer—weakened, multiplied, or reversed—into the other, affecting the shaping of subjectivity in that domain.

In my reception, Winnicott's space of play bears unexpected resemblances to Althusser's "ideology," which likewise exists only *in* and *for* subjects, which subjects produce and reproduce, which subjects occupy and activate at the same time that they remain the precipitates, vaguely separate, of it. I want for this homology to remain, especially insofar as Winnicott supplements Althusser by emphasizing the interior realm of subjectivity and the capacities subjects might have for intervening in social spaces—by "playing" with them and their contents, just as we might play with discourse and representation to shift the bounds of the categories that contain us.

Cultural criticism often sees its mission as being involved with the transformation, the reshaping, of subjects, or, in the case of much recent postmodernist theory, as tracing the reformation of subjects that is presumably happening under the transformative pressures of culture itself. Whether or not contemporary subjects are all becoming subject to the fractured, fragmented space described by Fredric Jameson or Gilles Deleuze is probably undecidable without considerable quantitative research, but perhaps the question is irrelevant anyway, given that their use of this language remains more metaphoric than descriptive. It can be demonstrated, however, as I have proved, that the phrase "the space of the subject" is not always or necessarily metaphorical, that subjectivity does indeed possess a shape, that different subjectivities have different spaces, and that the space of one particular subject or group of subjects can indeed change. Admittedly, the attempt to revise discourse to effect a conversion of the real is a slow and complicated process. And yet, in a few short decades, the words of women have markedly affected the worlds of the sexes, changing not only the place given women, socially and politically, or the places women can occupy, or the shape representations of women can take, but the shapes we, our very selves, are capable of taking. And that is hopeful observation indeed.

"Space" can give us the flexibility we need to capture all the multiple dimensions of subjectivity, while also providing the means for theorizing subjective mutability. We plot ourselves a destination, and inevitably find ourselves caught up in following the very outline we thought delimited ourselves.

Bibliography

Althusser, Louis. "Ideology and Idological State Apparatuses (Notes Towards an Investigation)." In *Lenin and Philosophy and Other Essays*, 127–186. Trans. Ben Brewster. New York: Monthly Review, 1971. Original published 1969.

Anzaldúa, Gloria. *Borderlands/La Frontera*. San Francisco: Spinsters/Aunt Lute Press, 1987.

Anzieu, Didier. *Le moi-peau*. Paris: Bordas-Dunod, 1985.

Baer, Judith. "Rape." *Encyclopedia of the American Justice System* vol. 3, 1252–1270. Ed. Robert J. Janosik. New York: Charles Scribner's Sons, 1987.

Baudrillard, Jean. *Simulations*. Trans. Paul Foss and Paul Patton. New York: Semiotext(e), 1983.

Benjamin, Jessica. *The Bonds of Love: Psychoanalysis, Feminism, and the Problem of Domination*. New York: Pantheon, 1988.

Benjamin, Walter. "On Some Motifs in Baudelaire." In *Illuminations*, 155–200. Ed. Hannah Arendt. Trans. Harry Zohn. New York: Schocken, 1968.

Benjamin, Walter. "Paris, Capital of the Nineteenth Century." In *Reflections: Essays, Aphorisms, Autobiographical Writings*, 146–162. Trans. Edmund Jephcott. New York: Schocken, 1986. Collection originally published 1978.

Berman, Marshall. *All that Is Solid Melts into Air: The Experience of Modernity*. New York: Penguin, 1982.

Bird, Jon, et al., eds. *Mapping the Futures: Local Cultures, Global Change*. Futures: New Perspectives for Cultural Analysis Series. New York: Routledge, 1993.

Bondi, Liz. "Locating Identity Politics." In *Place and the Politics of Identity*, 84–101. Ed. Michael Keith and Steve Pile. New York: Routledge, 1993.

Butler, Judith. *Gender Trouble: Feminism and the Subversion of Identity*. New
    York: Routledge, 1990.
Certeau, Michel de. *The Practice of Everyday Life*. Trans. Steven Rendall.
    Berkeley and Los Angeles: University of California Press, 1984.
Champlain, Samuel de. *Les Voyages du Sieur de Champlain*. Ann Arbor:
    University Microfilms, 1966.
Champlain, Samuel de. *Voyages of Samuel de Champlain 1604–1618*. Ed. W.
    L. Grant. Original Narratives of Early American History Series. New
    York: Scribners, 1907.
Chodorow, Nancy. *The Reproduction of Mothering: Psychoanalysis and the
    Sociology of Gender*. Berkeley and Los Angeles: University of California
    Press, 1978.
Cixous, Hélène. "Sorties." Trans. Ann Liddle. *New French Feminism: An
    Anthology*, 90–98. Ed. Elaine Marks and Isabelle de Courtivron. New
    York: Schocken, 1981. Original published 1975.
Colomina, Beatriz, ed. *Sexuality and Space*. Vol. 1 of Princeton Papers on
    Architecture. Princeton, NJ: Princeton Architectural Press, 1992.
Coward, Rosalind, and John Ellis. *Language and Materialism: Developments in
    Semiology and the Theory of the Subject*. London: Routledge and Kegan
    Paul, 1977.
Deleuze, Gilles, and Félix Guattari. *Anti-Oedipus: Capitalism and Schizophrenia*.
    1972. Trans. Robert Hurley, Mark Seem, and Helen R. Lane. Minne-
    apolis: University of Minnesota Press, 1983. Original published 1972.
Deleuze, Gilles, and Félix Guattari. *A Thousand Plateaus: Capitalism and
    Schizophrenia*, vol. 2. Trans. Brian Massumi. Minneapolis: University of
    Minnesota Press, 1987. Original published 1980.
Derrida, Jacques. "Différance." In *Margins of Philosophy*, 1–27. Trans. Alan
    Bass. Chicago: University of Chicago Press, 1982. Original published
    1972.
Descartes, René. *Meditations on First Philosophy*. In *Philosophical Writings*,
    160–248. Ed. and trans. Norman Kemp Smith. New York: Modern
    Library, 1958.
Doane, Mary Ann. "Film and Masquerade: Theorizing the Female Spectator."
    Screen 23, nos. 3–4 (1982): 74–87.
Doctor, Ronald M., and Ada P. Kahn. *The Encyclopedia of Phobias, Fears, and
    Anxieties*. New York: Facts on File, 1989.
Enelow, Morton L. "Public Nuisance Offenses: Exhibitionism, Voyeurism
    and Transvestism." In *Sexual Behaviour and the Law*, 478–486. Ed. Ralph
    Slovenko. Springfield, IL: Charles C. Thomas, 1965.
Foucault, Michel. *The Archaelogy of Knowledge*. Trans. A. M. Sheridan Smith.
    New York: Pantheon, 1972. Original published 1969.
Foucault, Michel. *Discipline and Punish: The Birth of the Prison*. Trans. Alan
    Sheridan. New York: Vintage/Random House, 1979. Original pub-
    lished 1975.
Foucault, Michel. *The Foucault Reader*. Ed. Paul Rabinow. New York:
    Pantheon, 1984.

Foucault, Michel. "The History of Sexuality." In *Power/Knowledge: Selected Interviews and Other Writings 1972–1977,* 183–193. Ed. Colin Gordon. Trans. Colin Gordon, Leo Marshall, John Mepham, and Kate Soper. New York: Pantheon, 1980.

Foucault, Michel. *The History of Sexuality, Volume 1: An Introduction.* Trans. Robert Hurley. New York: Vintage, 1980. Original published 1978.

Foucault, Michel. "On Popular Justice." In *Power/Knowledge: Selected Interviews and Other Writings 1972–1977,* 1–36. Ed. Colin Gordon. Trans. Colin Gordon, Leo Marshall, John Mepham, and Kate Soper. New York: Pantheon, 1980.

Freud, Sigmund. *Beyond the Pleasure Principle.* Ed. and trans. James Strachey. New York: Norton, 1961. Original publishd 1920.

Freud, Sigmund. *Civilization and Its Discontents.* Ed. and trans. James Strachey. New York: Norton, 1961. Original published 1930.

Freud, Sigmund. *The Ego and the Id.* In *The Standard Edition of the Works of Sigmund Freud,* vol. 19, 3–66. Ed. and trans. James Strachey. London: Hogarth Press, 1961. Original published 1923.

Fuss, Diana. *Essentially Speaking: Feminism, Nature and Difference.* New York: Routledge, 1989.

Gallop, Jane. *The Daughter's Seduction: Feminism and Psychoanalysis.* Ithaca, NY: Cornell University Press, 1982.

Gallop, Jane. *Reading Lacan.* Ithaca, NY: Cornell University Press, 1985.

Gregory, Derek. *Geographical Imaginations.* Cambridge, MA: Blackwell, 1994.

Gregory, Derek, and Rex Walford. *Horizons in Human Geography.* Totowa, NJ: Barnes and Noble, 1989.

Grosz, Elizabeth. "Space, Time and Bodies." Paper presented at the annual meeting of the International Association for Philosophy and Literature, Irvine, CA, April 27, 1990.

Harding, Sandra. *The Science Question in Feminism.* Ithaca: Cornell University Press, 1986.

Harley, J. B. "Deconstructing the Map." *Cartographica* 26, no. 2 (1989): 1–20.

Harley, J. B. "Silences and Secrecy: The Hidden Agenda of Cartography in Early Modern Europe." *Imago Mundi* 40 (1988): 57–76.

Harley, J. B. "Victims of a Map: New England Cartography and the Native Americans." Unpublished manuscript available through the Department of Geography at University of Wisconsin at Milwaukee.

Harvey, David. *The Condition of Postmodernity: An Enquiry into the Origins of Social Change.* Cambridge, UK: Basil Blackwell, 1989.

Harvey, David. "From Space to Place and Back Again: Reflections on the Condition of Postmodernity." In *Mapping the Futures: Local Cultures, Global Changes,* 3–29. Futures: New Perspectives for Global Analysis Series. Ed. John Bird et al. New York: Routledge, 1993.

Hawkesworth, Mary E. "Knowers, Knowing, Known: Feminist Theory and Claims of Truth." In *Feminist Theory in Practice and Process,* 327–351. Ed. Micheline R. Malson et al. Chicago: University of Chicago Press, 1989.

Helgerson, Richard. "The Land Speaks: Cartography, Chorography, and Subversion in Renaissance England." *Representations* 16 (1986): 51–85.

Herrmann, Claudine. "Women in Space and Time." Trans. Marilyn R. Schuster. In *New French Feminism: An Anthology,* 168–173. Ed. Elaine Marks and Isabelle de Courtivron. New York: Schocken, 1981. Original published 1976.

hooks, bell. *Feminist Theory: From Margin to Center.* Boston: South End Press, 1984.

Hooykaas, R. "The Rise of Modern Science: When and Why." *British Journal for the History of Science* 20 (1987): 453–473.

Irigaray, Luce. *This Sex Which Is Not One.* Trans. Catherine Porter. Ithaca, NY: Cornell University Press, 1985. Original published 1977.

Jameson, Fredric. "Cognitive Mapping." In *Marxism and the Interpretation of Culture,* 347–357. Eds. Cary Nelson and Lawrence Grossberg. Chicago: University of Illinois Press, 1988.

Jameson, Fredric. "Imaginary and Symbolic in Lacan." In *Literature and Psychoanalysis: The Question of Reading: Otherwise,* 338–395. Ed. Shoshana Felman. Baltimore: Johns Hopkins University Press, 1982.

Jameson, Fredric. "Postmodernism, or, the Cultural Logic of Late Capitalism." *New Left Review* 146 (1984): 53–92.

Jameson, Fredric. *Postmodernism, or, the Cultural Logic of Late Capitalism.* Durham, NC: Duke University Press, 1991.

JanMohamed, Abdul. "The Economy of Manichean Allegory: The Function of Racial Difference in Colonialist Literature." In *"Race," Writing and Difference,* 78–106. Ed. Henry Louis Gates, Jr. Chicago: University of Chicago Press, 1986.

Jardine, Alice A. *Gynesis: Configurations of Woman and Modernity.* Ithaca, NY: Cornell University Press, 1985.

Kaplan, E. Ann. "Is the Gaze Male?" In *Powers of Desire: The Politics of Sexuality,* 309–327. Ed. Ann Snitow, Christine Stansell, and Sharon Thompson. New York: Monthly Review Press, 1983.

Keith, Michael, and Steve Pile, eds. *Place and the Politics of Identity.* New York: Routledge, 1993.

Keller, Evelyn Fox. *The Science Question in Feminism.* Ithaca: Cornell University Press, 1986.

Kern, Stephen. *The Culture of Time and Space, 1880–1918.* Cambridge, MA: Harvard University Press, 1983.

Kipnis, Laura. "Feminism: the Political Conscience of Postmodernism?" In *Universal Abandon?* 149–167. Ed. Andrew Ross. Minneapolis: University of Minnesota Press, 1989.

Kristeva, Julia. *Powers of Horror: An Essay on Abjection.* Trans. Leon S. Roudiez. New York: Columbia University Press, 1982. Original published 1980.

Lacan, Jacques. "The Agency of the Letter in the Unconscious or Reason since Freud." In *Ecrits: A Selection,* 146–178. Trans. Alan Sheridan. New York: Norton, 1977. Original published 1957.

Lacan, Jacques. "Aggressivity in Psychoanalysis." In *Ecrits: A Selection,* 8–29.

Trans. Alan Sheridan. New York: Norton, 1977. Original published 1966.

Lacan, Jacques. *Feminine Sexuality.* Ed. Juliet Mitchell and Jacqueline Rose. Trans. Jacqueline Rose. New York: Norton, 1982. Chapters originally published separately, 1966, 1968, and 1975.

Lacan, Jacques. *The Four Fundamental Concepts of Psycho-Analysis.* Ed. Jacques-Alain Miller. Trans. Alan Sheridan. New York: Norton, 1977. Original published 1973.

Lacan, Jacques. "The Mirror Stage as Formative of the Function of I." In *Ecrits: A Selection,* 1–7. Trans. Alan Sheridan. New York: Norton, 1977. Original published 1949.

Lauretis, Teresa de. *Alice Doesn't: Feminism, Semiotics, Cinema.* Bloomington: Indiana University Press, 1984.

Lauretis, Teresa de. *Technologies of Gender: Essays on Theory, Film, and Fiction.* Bloomington: Indiana University Press, 1987.

Leibniz, Gottfried Wilhelm. *Philosophical Writings.* Ed. G.H.R. Parkinson. Trans. Mary Morris and G.H.R. Parkinson. London: Dent and Sons, 1973.

Mackinnon, Catharine A. "Desire and Power: A Feminist Perspective." In *Marxism and the Interpretation of Culture,* 105–116. Ed. Cary Nelson and Lawrence Grossberg. Urbana: University of Illinois Press, 1988.

Massey, Doreen. "Power-Geometry and a Progressive Sense of Place." In *Mapping the Futures: Local Cultures, Global Change,* 59–69. Futures: New Perspectives for Cultural Analysis Series. Ed. Jon Bird et al. New York: Routledge, 1993.

Mazey, Mary Ellen, and David R. Lee. *Her Space, Her Place: A Geography of Women.* Resource Publications in Geography. Washington, DC: Association of American Geographers, 1983.

McKinney's Consolidated Laws of New York, Annotated, Vol. 39: Penal Law. Practice Commentaries by William C. Donnino. St. Paul, MN: West, 1989.

Minh-ha, Trinh T. *Woman, Native, Other: Writing Postcoloniality and Feminism.* Bloomington: Indiana University Press, 1989.

Mohanty, Chandra Talpade. "Cartographies of Struggle: Third World Women and the Politics of Feminism." In *Third World Women and the Politics of Feminism,* 1–47. Ed. Chandra Talpade Mohanty. Bloomington: Indiana University Press, 1991.

Mohanty, Chandra Talpade. "Feminist Encounters: Locating the Politics of Experience." *Copyright* 1 (1987): 30–44.

Mohanty, Chandra Talpade, and Biddy Martin. "Feminist Politics: What's Home Got to Do with It?" In *Feminist Studies/Critical Studies,* 191–212. Ed. Teresa de Lauretis. Bloomington: Indiana University Press, 1986.

Morgan, Robin. "Planetary Feminism: The Politics of the 21st Century." In *Sisterhood is Global: The International Women's Movement Anthology,* 1–37. New York: Anchor Press/Doubleday, 1984.

Mukerji, Chandra. "A New World-Picture: Maps as Capital Goods for the

Modern World System." In *From Graven Images: Patterns of Modern Materialism,* 79–130. New York: Columbia University Press, 1983.

Mulvey, Laura. "Afterthoughts on 'Visual Pleasure and Narrative Cinema' Inspired by *Duel in the Sun.*" *Framework* 2 (1981): 12–15.

Mulvey, Laura. "Visual Pleasure and Narrative Cinema." *Screen* 16, no. 3 (1975): 6–18.

New York Supplement, Second Series, vol. 338. N.Y.S.2d. St. Paul, MN: West, 1973.

O'Gorman, Edmundo. *The Invention of America.* Bloomington: Indiana University Press, 1961.

Ortiz, Alicia Dujovne. "Buenos Aires (an Excerpt)." *Discourse* 8 (1986–1987), 74–82.

Page, Evelyn. *American Genesis: The Colonial Writing of the North.* Boston: Gambit, 1973.

Ploscowe, Morris. *Sex and the Law.* New York: Prentice-Hall, 1951.

Pollock, Griselda. *Vision and Difference: Femininity, Feminism, and the Histories of Art.* London: Routledge, 1988.

Powell, J. M. *Mirrors of the New World: Images and Image-Makers in the Settlement Process.* Studies in Historical Geography. Hamden, CT: Archon, 1977.

Pratt, Mary Louis. "Scratches on the Face of the Country; or, What Mr. Barrow Saw in the Land of the Bushmen." In *"Race," Writing, and Difference,* 138–162. Ed. Henry Louis Gates, Jr. Chicago: University of Chiago Press, 1986.

Pratt, Minnie Bruce. "Identity: Skin Blood Heart." In *Yours in Struggle: Three Feminist Perspectives on Anti-Semitism and Racism,* 11–63. Ed. Elly Bulkin, Minnie Bruce Pratt, and Barbara Smith. Brooklyn, NY: Long Haul Press, 1984.

Reagon, Bernice Johnson. "Coalition Politics: Turning the Century." In *Home Girls: A Black Feminist Anthology,* 356–368. Ed. Barbara Smith. New York: Kitchen Table/Women of Color Press, 1983.

Rich, Adrienne. "Notes toward a Politics of Location." In *Blood, Bread, and Poetry: Selected Prose, 1979–1985,* 210–231. New York: Norton, 1986.

Rose, Gillian. "Some Notes towards Thinking about the Spaces of the Future." In *Mapping the Futures: Local Cultures, Global Change,* 70–83. Futures: New Perspectives for Cultural Analysis Series. Ed. John Bird et al. New York: Routledge, 1993.

Rose, Jacqueline. "Sexuality in the Field of Vision." In *Sexuality in the Field of Vision, 224–233.* London: Verso, 1986.

Rosen, Ismond. "Looking and Showing." In *Sexual Behaviour and the Law,* 487–514. Ed. Ralph Slovenko. Springfield, IL: Charles C. Thomas, 1965.

Rouse, Roger. "Mexican Migration and the Social Space of Postmodernism." *Diaspora* 1 no. 1 (1991): 7–23.

Said, Edward W. "Representing the Colonized: Anthropology's Interlocutors." *Critical Inquiry* 15 (1989): 205–225.

Saldivar, Jose David, "Chicano Studies on the Border." *Working Paper* 2. Milwaukee: Center for Twentieth Century Studies, 1989–1990.

Schivelbusch, Wolfgang. *The Railway Journey: Trains and Travel in the Nineteenth Century.* Trans. Anselm Hollo. Oxford, UK: Basil Blackwell, 1980.

Sekula, Alan. "The Body and the Archive." *October* 39 (1986), 3–64.

Showalter, Elaine. "Feminist Criticism in the Wilderness." In *The New Feminist Criticism: Essays on Women, Literature, and Theory,* 243–270. Ed. Elaine Showalter. New York: Pantheon, 1985.

Silverman, Kaja. *The Acoustic Mirror: The Female Voice in Psychoanalysis and Cinema.* Bloomington: Indiana University Press, 1988.

Slovenko, Ralph. "A Panoramic View: Sexual Behavior and the Law." In *Sexual Behaviour and the Law,* 5–144. Ed. Ralph Slovenko. Springfield, IL: Charles C. Thomas, 1965.

Smith, Alexander B. and Harriet Pollack. *Some Sins Are Not Crimes: A Plea for Reform of the Criminal Law.* New York: Franklin and Watts—New Viewpoints, 1975.

Smith, Neil, and Cindi Katz. "Grounding Metaphor: Towards a Spatialized Politics." In *Place and the Politics of Identity,* 67–83. Ed. Michael Keith and Steve Pile. New York: Routledge, 1993.

Smith, Paul. *Discerning the Subject.* Theory and History of Literature, vol. 55. Minneapolis: University of Minnesota Press, 1988.

Soja, Edward W. *Postmodern Geographies: The Reassertion of Space in Critical Social Theory.* New York: Verso, 1989.

Soja, Edward, and Barbara Hooper. "The Spaces That Difference Makes: Some Notes on the Geographical Margins of the New Cultural Politics." In *Place and the Politics of Identity,* 183–205. Ed. Michael Keith and Steve Pile. New York: Routledge, 1993.

Spillers, Hortense. " 'An Order of Constancy': Notes on Brooks and the Feminine." In *Reading Black, Reading Feminist: A Critical Anthology,* 244–271. Ed. Henry Louis Gates, Jr. New York: Meridian, 1990.

Spivak, Gayatri. "Three Women's Texts and a Critique of Imperialism." In *Feminisms: An Anthology of Literary Theory and Criticism,* 798–814. Ed. Robyn R. Warhol and Diane Price Herndl. New Brunswick, NJ: Rutgers University Press, 1991.

Stephanson, Anders. "An Interview with Fredric Jameson" *Universal Abandon?* 3–30. Ed. Andrew Ross. Minneapolis: University of Minnesota Press, 1989.

Strategies 3 (1990).

Todorov, Tzvetan. *The Conquest of America: The Question of the Other.* Trans. Richard Horvard. New York: Harper and Row, 1984. Original published 1982.

Tuan, Y. F. *Topophilia: A Study of Environmental Perception, Attitudes, and Values.* Englewood Cliffs, NJ: Prentice-Hall, 1974.

Turner, Frederick. *Beyond Geography: The Western Spirit against the Wilderness.* New York: Viking, 1980.

Turner, Frederick Jackson. *The Frontier in American History*. New York: Holt, 1920. Original published 1893.
United States Supreme Court Digest 1754 to Date. Vols. 3, 9A, 10A. St. Paul, MN: West, 1953.
Vaca, Cabeza de. *Adventures in the Unknown Interior of America*. Trans. and ed. Cyclone Covey. Albuquerque: University of New Mexico Press, 1961.
Winnicott, D. W. *Playing and Reality*. New York: Basic Books, 1971.

Index